Praise for *Debt Trap Nation*

"An eye-opening and fascinating read from the very start. Debt is a subject not spoken about enough and this book reveals who's really to blame. Everybody should read this book." – Kwajo Tweneboa, campaigner, activist and author of *Our Country in Crisis*

"*Debt Trap Nation* is a chilling and eye-opening exposé on how the British state keeps some of the most vulnerable women in society trapped in a cycle of debt, homelessness and domestic violence. With clarity and compassion, this book gives voice to those living at the sharpest edge of austerity, and makes an irrefutable case for change." – Grace Blakeley, author of *Vulture Capitalism*

"Essential. A must-read." – Vicky Spratt, i Paper's Housing Correspondent and author of *Tenants*

"An urgent, illuminating book that lays bare just how deeply and devastatingly successive governments have let down those in need of a safe, secure place to live. The life-changing consequences for single mothers and children are harrowing; the cost of ignoring the stories and research uncovered by *Debt Trap Nation* is beyond measure." – Dan Hewitt, ITV News Investigations Editor

"*Debt Trap Nation* is a shocking account of England's hidden debt scandal, told through the eyes of families at the sharp end of a country in crisis." – Darren McGarvey, author of *Poverty Safari*

"Shocking, timely and terrifying. From ten-fold increases in rat infestations, to housing offered to homeless families with only bare floorboards, or worse, *Debt Trap Nation* illustrates what people – most usually women with young children – are made to put up with. And how they are milked dry of money first, often by private landlords, so that they have no choice but to accept the worse. It is a picture of a deteriorating state with its safety nets full of holes. At some point we will begin to change all this. That time is yet to come, and Brickell and Nowicki's book explains why sticking plasters and platitudes are not enough." – Danny Dorling, 1971 Professor of Geography, University of Oxford

"Equal parts sobering analysis and searing portrait, *Debt Trap Nation* brings readers face to face with the realities of family homelessness in England today while dissecting the systematic policy choices that produce it." – David Madden, Associate Professor in Sociology, London School of Economics

"An eviscerating study of the UK's failing welfare state and the systematic abandonment of vulnerable families to homelessness, squalor, ill-health and despair. *Debt Trap Nation* offers irrefutable evidence of why state investment in safe and affordable social housing is the only practicable solution to a deepening social crisis." – Imogen Tyler, Professor of Sociology, Lancaster University, and Fellow of the Academy of Social Sciences

"This wonderful book vividly captures the lived reality of poverty in the UK. It exposes the callousness and ignorance (not to mention misogyny) that all too often drives societal responses to the plight of single mothers and their children. A major achievement of the book is that it identifies crucial and feasible steps that could be taken to transform the lives of those affected as well as society itself." – Philip Alston, former UN Human Rights Council Special Rapporteur on extreme poverty and human rights, and John Norton Pomeroy Professor of Law, New York University

"The book serves as a beacon of hope by showing how reimagining policy could deliver economic justice. In this way it represents a compelling call to action." – Nicola Sharp-Jeffs OBE, founder of Surviving Economic Abuse

"A moving book with incisive analysis about structures and systems of indebtedness that subjugate the poor to lives of radical uncertainty. Especially important is Brickell and Nowicki's argument that such debt extends beyond homelessness, turning housing itself into a trap. For all those concerned with understanding and dismantling racial capitalism, this book is a must-read." – Ananya Roy, Professor of Urban Planning, Social Welfare and Geography, University of California Los Angeles

"Brickell and Nowicki powerfully capture the brutal everyday realities faced by a growing number of women and children caught in the violent grip of debt traps. Their cogent analysis is essential reading for anyone seeking to understand the inner workings of contemporary capitalism." – Susanne Soederberg, Canada Research Chair in Just and Inclusive Cities, Queen's University

"Incisive and clear, *Debt Trap Nation* shows how the interlinked crises of debt and homelessness are impacting the lives and wellbeing of single mothers and their children. This is an urgent call to action to end an increasingly punitive welfare system." – Alva Gotby, author of *Feeling at Home*

DEBT TRAP NATION

Family Homelessness in a Failing State

KATHERINE BRICKELL
AND
MEL NOWICKI

agenda
publishing

For everyone who has experienced homelessness

First published in 2025 by Agenda Publishing

Agenda Publishing Limited
PO Box 185
Newcastle upon Tyne
NE20 2DH

www.agendapub.com

ISBN 978-1-78821-864-1

British Library Cataloguing-in-Publication Data
A catalogue record for this book is available from the British Library

Typeset in Nocturne by Patty Rennie

Printed and bound in the UK by 4edge

EU GPSR authorised representative:
Logos Europe, 9 rue Nicolas Poussin, 17000 La Rochelle, France
contact@logoseurope.eu

Contents

Acknowledgements

First and foremost, we would like to thank our research participants, and the life experts we met along the way, for trusting us with your stories. You are the beating heart of this book, and we hope we've done justice to your experiences and the emotional energy we know it took to engage so deeply with us.

Thanks to everyone at the Shared Health Foundation, past and present, for all your support and inspiration, especially Sam Pratt and Jo Spurling. This book would not exist without you.

Thank you to Chris from Bison Bison (https://www.bisonbison.co.uk) for designing a cover to be proud of and that will hopefully encourage lots of people to pick up the book and learn more about women's vital stories. Di Boyle from Rooftop Illustrations (https://www.rooftopillustrations.net) worked with us closely to bring each chapter alive through her arresting and evocative illustrations. It has been a joy to work with you both.

At King's College London, special thanks goes to Fraser Curry, who painstakingly submitted Freedom of Information requests and collated social housing allocation policies for every local authority in England: no mean feat! You've been absolutely central to the later stages of this project, and we look forward to working together further. Thank you to the London Interdisciplinary Social Science Doctoral Training Partnership and its Research Assistant Internship Scheme for enabling this to happen.

The geographical research and engagement work underpinning *Debt Trap Nation* would not have been possible without support from the Urban Studies Foundation, British Academy, and King's Economic and Social Research Council Impact Acceleration Account. Special thanks to Felicity Mallam for helping us to get to the next phase of our work for the coming years, with support from Wates Family Enterprise Trust, Impact on Urban Health, People's Health Trust and Alan Morton.

Thanks to all our colleagues for their invaluable suggestions and advice. Ella Harris, our work together on family experiences of temporary accommodation in South London was the moment that started us on this journey nearly a decade ago. The Urban Futures Research Group in the Department of Geography at King's College London provided several rounds of feedback on different chapters that was hugely appreciated. Phillipa Williams at Queen Mary University of London helped us keep to time at the end of the writing process and gave invaluable feedback. We have also benefitted from presenting parts of the book internationally at the Goethe University Frankfurt, University of Zurich and Sapienza University of Rome, and in the UK at the Royal Geographical Society, Museum of the Home, Housing Studies Association, the Crisis Homelessness Summit and Shared Health Foundation Homeless Family Conferences.

Finally, warm thanks to our family and friends for their unwavering encouragement. Katherine would like to thank her parents, sister, husband, son and mother-in-law for the support needed to undertake this research and book. Katherine has been lucky to have wonderful cheerleaders along the way: thank you to Harriet, Ruth C., Sarah K., Ellen, Gail, Caroline, Ruth J., Ali and Jana. Mel would like to thank her parents, Toni and Vince, for inspiring her to always care about social injustice, to Jon for being an amazing partner and to Sacha for bringing a whole new level of meaning to everything. Thank you to Alice, Yvette, Harriet, Charlie and Hanne for their enduring friendship and reliable willingness to indulge a rant.

IT IS NOT WOMEN
WHO ARE FAILING,
WOMEN
ARE
BEING
FAILED
HOME

1

Debt trap nation

EVIE'S STORY

Fizzing sounds of sparklers and starbursts of gold danced across the screen of Evie's phone. These special effects embellished a video of her jangling keys outside her new front door. She hadn't known what to expect before moving into the freshly built social housing. It had to be accepted "sight unseen". But she'd been the lucky one, Evie thought as she stood there. Her friends couldn't say the same. With no alternatives offered, they had been forced to take social housing tenancies in areas they didn't know, and in properties full of mould, cracks and vermin. Some had gardens, but these were more like swamps than safe places for their children to play.

After proudly messaging the video to friends and family, Evie slid the phone into her pocket and took a moment to take in the surrealness of her hopes met. A place for her family to root, to grow, to rebuild after years of exhaustion – wedged into cramped hotel rooms and temporary flats with three children and all their belongings.

Evie turned the key in the lock and opened the door for the first time. She took off her shoes and stepped in. An icy coldness greeted her feet. The house had no flooring. In that moment, Evie had a flashback to a former tenancy with only stone-cold concrete. Her youngest son Josh smiling and running towards her. The fall on the hard stone floor. The broken tooth, the inconsolable cries she tried to comfort. Perhaps this new house was not the promised-for end of her journey through poverty, debt and mothering on the edge. Hard decisions would still have to be made. Go further into debt to pay for carpet, or keep going, with bare concrete floors and all the discomfort and likely injury they would bring? Not to mention the eye-watering heating bills that lack of adequate flooring would undoubtedly entail. And what about buying any furniture? White goods?[1] How was she going to be able to afford any of it? The list quickly corkscrewed into the pit of her stomach. The free-spirited sparkle she had allowed herself to momentarily feel was gone.

An alarm had started to shrill in Evie's pocket. It was time for the hour-long trip to her children's primary school. The daily fear that the second bus wouldn't arrive on time, and she'd be late again. A two-hour round trip, four hours of her day lost, every day. Becoming all too accustomed to being shunted between hotels at short notice, the children's original primary school was the sole place of stability left after becoming homeless and their father uncontactable. It was the only element of stability in their chaotic world, which Evie fiercely protected. The meals sacrificed to pay for the costs of travel seemed reluctantly the right call.

Evie's attempts to seek a job flexible enough to fit around the logistical demands of her children's schooling routine, and that paid enough to cover the costs of childcare, were getting nowhere. Her efforts felt like they were stuck on repeat, going around in ever more frustrated circles. Living in temporary accommodation for two years had been more than equivalent to a full-time job – caring on the move, advocating for their needs, and juggling their finances.

Strained still further by the rising cost of living, there was no room for manoeuvre given the diminished value of the welfare benefits she received. No flexibility to meet their basic needs. More long term than this, government decision-making to reduce public sector debt through austerity, including introducing the two-child benefit cap and defunding local services, had worsened the family's financial situation and health.

Living in radical uncertainty, to have moved the children between schools each time they were given notice on their latest temporary accommodation seemed foolish and irresponsible. She had to make it work. Evie had known pragmatically that it would be a long path to a secured social housing tenancy, which she now finally had. They were so scarce that her local authority had admitted publicly that with tens of thousands of families bidding and a severe lack of stock, under the current conditions it would take more than a century to find homes for everyone. Thatcher's Right to Buy scheme in the 1980s had ignited the mass selling of social housing in England, with much of it falling into the credit-fuelled hands of private landlords. There simply wasn't enough social housing left to go round.

Even if social housing was available, there were obstructive rules blocking the path to access. At one stage, Evie was even barred by her local authority from bidding for a social housing tenancy. She was trapped living in temporary accommodation because of the local authority's housing allocation scheme, which disqualified prospective tenants with "housing-related debts" totalling more than £1,000. Until she could repay £250 of her £1,250 rental arrears, even having a bidding number was out of the question.

The bad economics of it made no sense to her. What was £250 compared to the council paying a private landlord for the poor quality temporary accommodation she was stuck in at the time? Let alone the inhumanity of holding her in limbo because of rent arrears that were not even of her own making? Reports of local authorities risking bankruptcy because of the spiralling costs of temporary accommodation seemed to pop up in the news more and more. Perhaps the rule existed, she wondered, just to punish her? To keep her in a new-age debtors' prison? Temporary accommodation had certainly felt like a prison.

As Evie sat on the first bus to school, the financial stresses that were the foundation of her chronic insomnia coursed through her nervous system. She needed to repay the outstanding rent arrears owed to her private rented sector landlord, plus other loans. Before her relationship with long-term partner Lewis ended and they were evicted, the landlord had put the rent up. The cost of the landlord servicing his buy-to-let empire had increased and his borrowing costs were passed directly on to his tenants.

At the very same time that the rent jumped sky high, Evie's then partner turned the screws further on her financial worries. For several years Lewis had controlled her access to money, intentionally making Evie dependent on him, even for essentials such as food and clothing. When she challenged his behaviour, he retaliated by hitting her. When she called the police for help, they failed to take any action and Evie never called again. With Evie's freedom limited, and concerned how she would be able to financially cope outside of the relationship, she tried to carry on.

The rent increase was the precursor to Lewis stopping his financial contributions, and he secretly applied for loans in Evie's name using an app on her phone.

Rent arrears amassed, the family were evicted, and Lewis simply disappeared. Evie was left homeless, caring for their three children alone, coping with the trauma of domestic abuse and nursing multiple debts in a failing state.[2]

*

Evie's story is the story of *Debt Trap Nation.*

In the English dictionary, a trap is defined as something that prevents escape. It typically allows entry but not exit. It catches hold and does not let fully go. It works against the interests of those trapped. Evie's journey, told briefly here, is an immediate yet intimate entry point into household debt as a complex trap that families are becoming adversely caught in. *Debt Trap Nation* tells the stories of single mothers with dependent children in England who have experienced rent arrears and other forms of private debt, homelessness and living in temporary accommodation.

Evie's children were among the 164,000 children who were homeless and living in temporary accommodation in England at the time of writing.[3] Altogether, they would fill The O2 arena eight times over. The short and long-lasting detriments of problem debt and homelessness on children's development, health and education are eye-opening and tell a damning story of England. Through mothers' experiences, the book reveals how debt is not only causing and lengthening homelessness but also outliving it. In what follows, we trace their journeys, uncovering how families have not simply fallen into a debt trap but have been *pulled into* it. Railing against societal perception and stigma that associates being in debt and being homeless with personal failure, we flip the script. It is not women who are failing, women are being failed.

Although many individual elements of the debt trap we explore are experienced by a range of groups, we argue that their cumulative effect is felt most acutely by mothers – low-income single mothers particularly. Motherhood remains dominant in understandings of home, homemaking and caregiving in both policymaking and popular culture.[4] Despite this, not enough attention has been paid to the ways in which social policy conversely hampers women's ability to provide safe and secure homes for their children. Mothers are consistently framed in social policy terms as "protectors", meaning they are primarily responsible for the security and well-being of their children.[5] In turn, these long-standing cultural assumptions that regard motherhood as natural, instinctive and innate are used to legitimize punitive policies and justify the absence of supportive ones related to parenthood. For example, the two-child benefit cap and unaffordable and inflexible childcare systems both deeply undermine mothers' financial security and independence.[6] They hinder mothers and their children from finding a way out of the debt trap.

Systemic failings to support motherhood are by and large ignored in government policy. Instead, women's struggles to afford to care for their children or provide them with a decent and secure home are repackaged as the failings of unfit mothers. This problematic framing was made explicit in the 2010s by then Prime Minister David Cameron. In 2011, against the backdrop of his austerity agenda, Cameron launched the "Troubled Families Programme", which aimed to reduce "demand and dependency of these complex families on costly reactive public services and delivering better value for the taxpayer".[7] The programme's messaging was clear: low-income, unemployed and single mothers are a burden on the hardworking taxpayer. Even today, the signs do not bode well in terms of addressing these unfair characterizations. The Labour government's first Autumn Budget in October 2024 failed to remove the two-child benefit cap; if scrapped, 250,000 children would have been lifted out of poverty immediately.[8] That this rule was originally put in place and has remained so is repugnant.[9] Four and a half million children in the UK currently live in poverty.[10] A core aim of *Debt Trap Nation*, then, is to reveal the economic and moral callousness of blame placed on low-income, unemployed and single mothers. Mothers who are, in fact, being failed by some of the very systems that claim to protect them.

The women whose stories we learned about through our research in Greater Manchester and London represent just a fraction of the mothers in England facing problem debt and homelessness. They are bearing the brunt of debt distress, family homelessness and domestic abuse, the insidious impacts of austerity, and the cost-of-living crisis that has seen inflation and interest rates rise rapidly. This increased cost of living was triggered in part by the Covid-19 pandemic and the war on Ukraine, but it has been undoubtedly worsened by welfare systems and public services already decimated by over a decade of deep cuts. Labour Chancellor of the Exchequer Rachel

Reeves has repeatedly referred to a £22 billion "black hole" left by the preceding Conservative government, wielding it as a warning to the public that further savings will be needed to reduce national debts through welfare cuts.[11] In the run-up to the 2025 spring statement, Reeves publicly rejected analysis by the Joseph Rowntree Foundation (JRF) that showed the government were on course to fail in their milestone of raising living standards by the end of the current parliament. The JRF modelled that by April 2030 households will be £1,400 worse off on average than they are today, in part because of rising housing costs.[12] The statement delivered by Reeves emphasized once again the prioritization of "working people" (mentioning this phrase 16 times) and confirmed cuts planned to health and disability benefits.[13] This is despite the Department for Work and Pensions' own impact assessment indicating that more than 50,000 children and 250,000 people will be pushed into relative poverty by 2030 as a result of these cuts.[14] Others, including Duncan Shrubsole, chief executive of homelessness charity St Martin-in-the-Fields, voiced concern that cuts will only result in increased homelessness.[15] The chief executive of the JRF, Paul Kissack, also responded with incredulity that: "with living standards for the poorest under continuing assault, the government needs to protect people from harm with the same zeal as it attempts to build its reputation for fiscal competence".[16]

Some of the most vulnerable mothers, especially those that are lone parents and on the lowest incomes, are at the sharp end of such government decisions and fiscal disciplining. StepChange Debt Charity's *Statistics Yearbook* for 2024 shows that over a quarter (27 per cent) of their clients are single parents, despite only accounting for 7 per cent of families in the wider UK population.[17] Data from the charity also reveal that 64 per cent of people seeking their debt advice are women. They are disproportionately affected by debt given the gender pay gap, employment gaps, cuts to benefits and welfare spending, caring responsibilities and domestic abuse, including economic abuse.[18] Nationally, 60 per cent of all homeless adults in temporary accommodation are women.[19] Mothers who are lone parents are particularly at risk. Government figures show that for July to September 2024, 16 per cent of all households in England owed a homeless "relief duty" (assistance) from a local authority were female parents with dependent children. According to Shelter's 2021 *Fobbed Off* report, 1 in 38 lone mothers in England are homeless, and a shocking one in three are in arrears or struggling to keep a roof over their head. In London these homelessness statistics are especially bad – 65 per cent of adult occupiers in temporary accommodation are women and 37 per cent of homeless households in temporary accommodation are headed by single mothers.[20] The cost-of-living crisis is exacerbating the threat of debt for this group even further, with 37 per cent of single mothers' financial situations worsening between 2022 and 2023.[21]

Another key contributor to the debt trap is domestic abuse – again disproportionately affecting women and mothers like Evie. Approximately 1.6 million women are experiencing domestic abuse,[22] and 18.6 per cent of victims are lone parents.[23] Support continues to be limited, and the police have shattered public trust both in their systematic mishandling of domestic abuse cases and through the violent actions of officers themselves, including the kidnap, rape and murder of Sarah Everard by a serving police officer in 2021. According to government reporting, as of 2024 fewer than half of domestic abuse cases in England and Wales end up as police-recorded crimes, and when they do, the vast majority of cases do not end with prosecutions.[24] Even if women do turn to the police for help, they are met with chronically inadequate support, and it is not unusual for their experiences to be disbelieved and belittled. As we highlight in detail later, domestic abuse and homelessness are deeply intertwined. Around 16 per cent of households in England present as homeless to local authorities as a direct result of domestic abuse.[25]

State failings to ensure women's safety inside and outside of the home are held up by patriarchal values that facilitate and normalize their disempowerment. They also combine with neoliberal ideology that dictates free market principles as central to a successful society, despite mounting evidence to the contrary. These belief systems have contributed to the implementation of long-term austerity policies, establishing a political landscape that neglects the needs of vulnerable women and unleashes gender-based violence through macroeconomic policy decisions that harm them physically, emotionally and psychologically.[26] It has become normalized to dismiss and devalue the experiences of women suffering from domestic abuse, and to problematize single mothers in debt as irresponsible, rather than acknowledge the multiple systemic issues at play. As a past deputy cabinet secretary disclosed, "thinking about how people will be impacted and planning to minimise harm is a professional skill that is chronically undervalued in the machinery of government".[27] This institutionalized lack of empathy is central to enabling the debt trap.

The moral shortcomings of governments unwilling to consider or mitigate the harms of its own decision-making is arresting. To quote Nelson Mandela, speaking in 1995, "There can be no keener revelation of a society's soul than the way in which it treats its children".[28] If the numbers continue to grow at the rate they have been, by December 2030 there could be nearly 400,000 children in temporary accommodation, deprived of a basic sense of safety and stability.[29] Worse still, our research has found that most local authority housing allocation policies actively penalize households like Evie's who have been made homeless as a consequence of rent arrears. Some do so through preventing indebted households, including mothers with dependent children, from applying for social housing that would alleviate some of their financial burden and enable them to move out of temporary accommodation. Local housing authorities use temporary accommodation to meet their statutory obligations to provide a roof to qualifying persons. In the UK this could be hotels, Bed and Breakfasts, private hostels, short-stay Houses in Multiple Occupation, or other emerging forms of provision such as modular developments, shipping containers, and converted office blocks.

England-wide research we pursued has uncovered, for the first time ever, that in December 2023 alone well over a thousand households with children living in temporary accommodation were deemed ineligible for a social housing tenancy because of outstanding housing-related debts. Not only is the true figure likely to be much higher, but these numbers will include mothers who have incurred debts because of economic coercion and abuse from ex-partners and/or have had to take on new debts to flee violent perpetrators. The debt trap is not only catching adults but also children.

Angela Rayner, the deputy prime minister and housing secretary, was not wrong in the first month of her tenure in 2024 when she said that the numbers of homeless children is a "national scandal" that reflected "the most acute housing crisis in living memory". Her diagnosis was that "there are simply not enough homes", a statement that is plainly correct, yet which hides many of the complexities of why families are becoming homeless.[30] Problem debt is one such complexity that has been too often lacking in national debate on the housing crisis. It is an omission that we directly challenge. Children and their mothers are being left, literally, out in the cold, homeless through the accrual of debt and difficulties of repaying it in an economy that is working against them.

Rayner and other Labour ministers have rightly acknowledged the scandal of soaring homelessness in one of the world's wealthiest nations. And yet, they are currently not doing enough to acknowledge the role that government policies – national and local – play in this scandal, particularly when it comes to debt. Government debt collection practices are some of the worst, and are often far more punitive than private debtors. For example, dependent on the local authority, households grappling with the payment of council tax can be met with harsh punishment, including prison if "wilful refusal" or "culpable neglect" is established.[31] According to research conducted by the Money and Mental Health Policy Institute, founded by finance guru Martin Lewis, council tax debt collection policies are some of the most brutal in the country, far more so than the private debt sector.[32] One missed council tax payment can lead to a demand for the full annual council tax bill (averaging in a bill of £1,668 after just three weeks of non-payment). The institute's report also found that the regular use of enforcement agencies leaves people feeling terrified and powerless, hugely impacting their mental health. This is particularly concerning considering that people with mental health problems are more than twice as likely to be behind on council tax payments in the first place.

Women are also disproportionately affected, as they are more likely to have council tax bills in their name, meaning they remain liable for any missed payments, even after fleeing their home because of domestic abuse. This is far from the only instance of highly punitive state debt collection. The "cliff-edge" of carers allowance has been particularly controversial as it pushes many unpaid carers into tens of thousands of pounds of debt. In 2024–5, it was reported that more than 9,000 carers looking after their ill and disabled family members and loved ones were faced with debts of up to £20,000.[33] Highly punitive rules mean that if carers earn just £1 over a £151 weekly threshold for paid work, they can be charged in excess of £4,250 per year.[34] In May, the *Guardian* newspaper reported that Oksana Shahar, who cares for her autistic son, was left with debts of £10,000 after breaching

Department of Work and Pensions earning limits by an average of just £1.92 a week. Those with overpayment debts exceeding £5,000 are also threatened with potential criminal prosecution. All this is being enacted on a group of people who are undertaking essential social care work at a time of stressed health and welfare services.

The state's relationship with debt can be described as no less than an economic and political mess. Local authorities especially are spurred on to enact these harmful debt collection practices by their own indebtedness. A 2025 report by the National Audit Office revealed that almost half of all councils in England risk falling into bankruptcy as a consequence of a £4.6 billion deficit amassed across 14 years of Conservative governments.[35] Between 2010 and 2023, local government debt increased by 78 per cent, as councils themselves have increasingly turned to creditors to fill these cavernous gaps created by central government funding cuts.[36] Rather than instil empathy into local authority approaches, this tandem relationship with debt appears to have only hardened some of their responses to individuals struggling to make council tax payments. Combined, punitive social housing allocation schemes and council tax debt collection policies are evidence of a state that is failing some of its most vulnerable citizens.

How meaningful can promises of more social housebuilding be when thousands of homeless families are being actively banned from accessing it? This is a failure not only of economics but of compassion and imagination. The contribution of *Debt Trap Nation* lies in holding up a mirror to a nation steeped in debt and plunged into homelessness, a new-found realization that for all the necessary cries for more social housing, too much is broken for this to be the hoped for silver bullet. In response, we raise a series of crucial questions. What is the debt trap? How was it set? Who is being disproportionally trapped and why? And what can be done to escape it?

In this book we explore how the past 50 years of neoliberalism in England has produced and harmed families burdened with problem debt and housing insecurity. The so-called neoliberal turn of the 1970s refers to the beginning of an ideological shift whereby state funding of, and ownership over, essential services such as utilities, transport and housing were "rolled back". Spearheaded by infamous former Prime Minister Margaret Thatcher, so began an era of mass privatization, deregulation and the stigmatization of welfare recipients. This was not an inevitable shift, nor one that is irreversible. It was, and remains, the consequence of active decision-making by successive governments since Thatcher's that have prioritized enabling private profit for the few over welfare security for the many.

Decades of subsequent national over-reliance on credit, debt and unscrupulous, unregulated industries has not resulted in any *mea culpa* moments on the part of governments that the neoliberal project might be a failed one. Instead, responsibility has time and again been repackaged and blame assigned to those at the bottom of the economic chain. Blame is laid at the door – even when they no longer have one – of those with the least power and resources to counter the dominant narrative: that the country's economic and social failings are not the consequence of mass privatization or mismanaged finances but the result of the "work-shy", single mothers and "troubled" and "broken" families. This narrative puts the onus on the most vulnerable to help themselves, to work harder, to spend less, according to housing activist Kwajo Tweneboa. But, he explains, in reality "these things won't resolve the decades of neglect and active damage the leaders of our country have wrought. But they don't want us to look at them; they'd rather punch downwards and blame intangible things beyond their control".[37]

One of the ways in which national governments past and present have shifted fiscal responsibility onto individuals is through framing and measuring economic productivity primarily in relation to paid work. This is a misguided disservice to the work of raising children, part of an entrenched misogyny (as an outcome of patriarchy) that has long dismissed the integral role of social reproduction (the bearing and raising of children, maintenance of households and sustaining of paid, typically male, labour). But such framing is particularly ironic when benefit and childcare policies can actively block mothers like Evie from accessing paid work. According to data from PricewaterhouseCoopers, the gender pay gap in the UK has widened four times faster than the average for Organisation for Economic Co-operation and Development (OECD) countries.[38] Women on low incomes were also found in their analysis to be more likely to quit their jobs after having children because the cost of childcare outstrips their income. This was certainly an issue we encountered time and again among the women we have interviewed. Despite increasingly well-documented state failures to provide affordable childcare, single mothers not in work continue to be blamed, rather than understood as being caught in an impossible bind. In his speech at the 2024 Labour Party Conference, newly elected Prime Minister Keir Starmer did nothing to steer the emphasis away from celebrating working people, implicitly framing those not in paid employment as societal failures. In his inaugural conference speech as prime minister, he made promises to serve "working people" (like the chancellor) upwards of 15 times.[39] Supporting low-income mothers and reforming childcare were conversely absent from his espousals of a better future for the country. This needs to change. Many of the mothers we spent time with dream of pursuing careers that would fulfil them, yet they face multiple barriers that are out of their control. Several were, in fact, in work but dealing with everything that comes with being homeless meant continuing simply wasn't possible. Still, they are deemed to be the ones at fault.

One of the driving motivations of this book is to call for the reassignment of this blame game. Families' lives, and their futures, are caught in a debt trap not of their making. Through recent economic history and political decision-making up to the present day, the trap in England has been "set". Geographer Danny Dorling depicts a country in which people feel "shattered", millions of households burdened by escalating levels of debt just to keep going, while the wealthy only see their fortunes soar.[40] *Debt Trap Nation* connects the dots through politicizing debt and mapping the connections between national and household debts in monetary *and* non-monetary terms. It also participates in the strategic feminist task of tracing the links between debt and misogynistic violence.

As Evie bitterly found out, a debt trap is a vicious cycle that is difficult to escape from, especially when the conditions for initial capture and continued captivity persist. Evie's debt was burdensome and problematic, even after moving into permanent social housing. Given that borrowing in the present is facilitated through repayment in the future, even when this housing is secured, debt and its punitive impacts can linger and accumulate still further. Credit mutates into debt the moment after it is borrowed, a haunting certainty and vicious cycle that Evie did not want to entertain again as she stepped onto the chilly floor of her new home. The carpet that was needed would once again require borrowing, if she was still credit-"worthy" to borrow. While carpet and its cost in economic and human terms might seem too banal and inconsequential to consider in the masculinist world of high finance, we argue in this book that the "little things" *matter*. The feminist orientation we take in the pages that follow allows the rethinking of what matters and whose life "counts" in the nation's calculus. How much debt is a child's chipped tooth worth taking on? This is one of the thousands of absurd calculations that families across England are essentially forced to make in a failing state *every day*.

This singular example encapsulates the contradictions of debt: on the one hand sustaining and augmenting domestic and family life, and on the other hand cruelly undermining and harming it. Such ambivalence is especially prescient for homeless single mothers, as state failings in providing enough support for low-income families means that taking on debt is part and parcel of everyday life-making. In asking what a debt trap is, and journeying into its dynamics together, we show how this is far from a simple story of economics. The debt trap goes beyond traditional parameters of "the economy". In this conception, we owe our own debt to the work of the late David Graeber, who in *Debt: The First 5,000 Years* writes:

> What is being shunted out of sight... is first of all the fact that *everyone* is in debt... and that very little of this debt was accrued by those determined to find money to bet on the horses or toss away on fripperies. Insofar as it was borrowed for what economists like to call discretionary spending, it was mainly to be given to children, to share with friends, or otherwise to be able to build and maintain relations with other human beings that are based on *something* other than sheer material calculation. One must go into debt to achieve a life that goes in any way beyond sheer survival... ultimately it's sociality itself that's treated as abusive, criminal, demonic.[41]

As captured here, the carpet that Evie was mulling buying on credit is not a decision based on indulgence or showiness but rather a purchase to avoid the hurt and unhomeliness of accommodations past. Her prospective borrowing arises from the lack of government funding for flooring and the standard practice of removing carpets between tenants in social housing. Evie is not alone in what she faces; the charity End Furniture Poverty estimate there to be 760,000 adults (9 per cent of all adult social tenants) living in social housing without floor coverings.[42] Even where local authorities do provide social housing – the supposed happy ending for those who have had to live through homelessness – the basic requirements for a safe and secure home aren't necessarily in place. In Evie's case, as with hundreds of thousands of others, a roof may have been provided but a home has not. A sense of feeling at home can also remain elusive, both financially and emotionally, as families battle living without the basics. This amounts to a "life of chronic denial":[43] a constancy of risk calculations characterize the experiences of indebted homeless families in the present day.

Debt Trap Nation is essentially a Machiavellian tale of ascribing guilt for England's household debt mountain and economic malaise to its low-income or "workless" populace already suffering multiple disadvantages and barriers. Family homelessness is a cause and consequence of inequality baked into our political and economic system. It is hitting women, particularly single mothers and people from racialized groups the hardest. Instead of focusing our critical gaze onto government and the private sector interests that have captured much of the machinery of the state, we are told to "look over there!" towards strained borrowers who are the ones that need to "pull their socks up".[44] We reject this political deflection strategy. What is needed is greater public critique of capitalism and the state's promotion of it through the privileging of private property and corporate interests, and the use of free (women's) labour to subsidize the costs of care that sustains families and workers (as traditionally defined) in the economy. Directing kindness to, and learning from, mothers and their children carrying the burden of England's more-than-housing crisis is a vital part of this pushback.

Taking on this task, we venture into the lives of families like Evie's to examine a state that is denying their rights to home and protection from harm. Preceding each chapter are stand-alone testimonies told by Christine, Sam and Jenna: all mothers who have each navigated homelessness with their children in different parts of the country, north and south. They choose to make their stories public through "life expert" talks and other means, to raise awareness of family homeless in England.[45]

What follows is a highly personal and politically energized reading of a failing state in technicolour.[46] No area of policy failure is left spared. Housing.

Welfare. Employment. Health and social care. Justice and law. Education. Transport. The book exposes the self-deception that the housing crisis can be solved solely by building more social housing. Yes, social housing supply is a, if not *the*, priority. Yes, the Labour Party are right to commit, as they have done in June 2025, to spending £39 billion on a social and affordable housing programme. Social housing is a non-negotiable in unlocking the debt trap, but it is not enough to dismantle it altogether. *Debt Trap Nation* points to other economic, societal and symbolic changes that are also needed to make a difference in low-income single mothers' lives and those of their children. Over the course of the book, we pull back the curtain on the country's debt trap and take you inside the domestic lives of those being adversely caught in its gravitational pull.

YOU'RE STUCK IN A DOOM LOOP

2

Not at home in a failing state

What is the debt trap? How was it set? Who is being disproportionally trapped and why? And what can be done to escape it? These are the questions at the heart of this book. In this chapter, we start to probe at state failures that have pulled families into problem debt and homelessness. They are being made to feel, and physically be, ***not at home*** in a failing state.

England is a country where international law is being flouted. The Universal Declaration of Human Rights codifies the right to adequate housing in which a range of freedoms are granted: protection against forced evictions; the right to be free from arbitrary interference with one's home, privacy and family; and the right to choose one's residence, to determine where to live and to freedom of movement.[1] These rights are, however, being systematically infringed, especially for women and children in England today. In the nineteenth and early twentieth centuries, "women and children first" was the prevailing norm in emergencies when survival resources were limited. In the early twenty-first century, when fiscal policy has shrunk the welfare state and the housing emergency is the worst in living memory, "women and children last" is the modus operandi. The debt trap has underlying unhoming tendencies that are being faced, head-on, by growing numbers of homeless families living in "temporary accommodation" that is anything but temporary.

As we alluded to earlier, not only are mothers and their children living in temporary accommodation being failed, but low-income single mothers are being belittled, stigmatized and blamed as "work-shy" citizens responsible for the country's impoverished economic and moral trajectory. They are being, like the population at large, "gaslit" – as several of our research participants put it – for failings that are not theirs to own. In this chapter we work to redress this trickery. We enter the mechanics of the debt trap to show what women and society at large are up against: the unavoidability of debt and its capacity to uproot families, engineer a monopoly of blame centred on debtors, harm mothers and their children physically and emotionally and imprison them in temporary accommodation, all the while extracting profit from their suffering. This recognition work is important for making the case, ultimately, that the debt trap warrants tearing down.

The unavoidable everyday of debt

A trap tends to be something difficult to avoid or something ultimately unavoidable. The underlying reasons for its existence have not been prevented, entrapment is inevitable and exit is hard to obtain. The systematic unfairness and economic failings of England's neoliberal trajectory since the late 1970s have left more and more families in such unavoidable problem debt. StepChange Debt Charity and the Children's Society use the term "debt trap" in relation to "problem debt": "where families have no option but to take on credit to pay for essentials, but the costs of keeping up debt repayments leads to further pressure on household budgets, so children miss out on the basics".[2] Debt Justice report that nearly ten million people in the UK are unable to pay their bills on time or are heavily burdened by debt repayments they are finding difficult to repay.[3] Further to this, "negative budgets", where people's basic outgoings (including debt repayments) cannot be covered by their income, are becoming more widespread, including for a greater number of people in full-time employment.[4] In 2024, the Financial Conduct Authority reported that 28 per cent (14.6 million) of adults weren't coping financially or finding it difficult to cope financially; 14 per cent (7.4 million) felt burdened by domestic bills and credit commitments; and 5 per cent (5.5 million) in the previous six months had missed paying these bills. A higher proportion of single adults with a financial dependent were found to be struggling.[5]

In other words, families can end up being sucked deeper into the debt trap through the burdens of repayment and a growing disparity between income and essential outgoings. In the absence of sufficient social protection, debt encloses lives and places, squeezing repayment out of bodies and homes until they yield. That households often have no option but to turn to credit, or run up rental arrears to sustain their everyday lives, is part of the ubiquitous everyday of debt that characterizes the present day. Debt is regularly described by charities, organizations and the press as "unavoidable".[6]

But in all of this, it is important to impress that the debt trap is not inevitable, it is a political choice. The debt trap is politically orchestrated. It has been constructed to catch and retain low-income working-class people in its grip. This is because debt is part of a governance shift to individualized and marketized forms of responsibilization, even for basic subsistence needs. Debt has become a requirement of survival to keep afloat. It is a form of what Susanne Soederberg calls "debtfare" in neoliberal times.[7] "Debtfare" consists of the increased reliance of the poor on debt for social reproduction – the sustaining of lives on a daily and generational basis – in the context of declining state support for welfare and housing. Although high-income households are the most likely to be in debt (largely through mortgages and other large-scale loans), it is low-income households in England who are most likely to be saddled with problem debt and are missing the payment of bills and credit commitments.[8]

Growing dependency on credit and heightened risk of arrears over the last 15 years are intimately connected to the governmental pursuit of austerity: the attempted reduction of public sector debt since 2010. The weight of public debt at this moment is associated with the 2008 global financial crisis, which saw the taxpayer bail out the banks with public money.[9] The economic narrative of this time, however, was almost immediately rewritten by government policy. Under the austerity agenda that followed, the postwar welfare state was eroded beyond recognition, with punitive measures towards benefits claimants being an explicit approach taken by successive governments since 2010. This agenda was set in motion by the 2012 Welfare Reform Act, which overhauled much of the welfare system. The Act included stringent targets to declare people fit for work, mandatory contributions to council tax regardless of income and reductions in housing benefits for social tenants deemed to have spare bedrooms (commonly known as the bedroom tax). Such policy shifts were instrumental in emphasizing state dependence as a marker of shame.

However, despite the common narrative of people on benefits being "work-shy", 38 per cent of people on Universal Credit (the amalgamated benefits system introduced in 2013) are in work.[10] A £20 uplift in Universal Credit payments was introduced in 2020 to provide extra support for people during the Covid-19 pandemic, but this was cut at the end of 2021, despite warnings that it would immediately pull an extra 500,000 people into poverty, including 200,000 children. This amounted to the biggest overnight cut to the basic rate of social security since the Second World War. Alongside the long shadow of the Covid-19 pandemic, 2022 saw inflation reach a 40-year high and trigger a cost-of-living crisis that hit people like Evie hard. According to the British Retail Consortium, food inflation was 16.8 per cent in December 2022, with budget supermarket ranges rising by 20.3 per cent in the same period.[11] Food inflation continues to rise. In the year to January 2025, inflation rose at its fastest pace in ten months, with cooking staples such as olive oil rising in cost by 17 per cent.[12] Energy prices have also skyrocketed, with average gas prices rising by 141 per cent and electricity prices by 65 per cent in winter 2021–22 alone. There have been falls in prices since, but as of December 2024 energy bills are still 43 per cent higher than 2021–22 levels.[13] These rising costs are not felt equally. It is the poorest 10 per cent of households nationally that spend 11 per cent of their income on energy, while this figure is only 4 per cent for the richest 10 per cent of households.[14] It is unsurprising given this "poverty tax" that debt advice charities are reporting an increase in clients in need of help with their debts. An Office for National Statistics survey showed that, of the 94 per cent of adults who saw an increase in their cost of living in December 2022, 22 per cent reported using more credit than usual to make ends meet.[15] A nationally representative survey from StepChange Debt Charity of 2000 UK consumers found that the single most common cause of problem debt in the UK in March 2025 was not alcohol, drugs or gambling, as is so often and wrongly assumed, but rather the cost-of-living increase.[16]

In spite of people's worsening financial conditions, governments, Conservative and Labour alike, have continued to justify punitive economic policies through such misconceptions of debt and the stigmatization of poverty. The continuing and attritional harms of austerity have been described by Imogen Tyler in her brilliant book *Stigma: The Machinery of Inequality* as a regime of fiscal discipline and proxy for "class war": "a war of breathtaking cruelty waged against the poorest, the most disadvantaged and vulnerable members of British society".[17] In 2018, the then United Nations (UN) Special Rapporteur on extreme poverty and human rights, Philip Alston, noted with similar conviction that "the experience of the United Kingdom, especially since 2010, underscores the conclusion that poverty is a political choice. Austerity could easily have spared the poor, if the political will had existed to do so."[18] Instead, he remarks, many already in crisis have been pushed into debt, rent arrears and serious hardship. At the press conference where Alston presented his findings verbally, he reflected in a sober tone on his interactions during the visit:

> What has surprised me is that there is close to unanimity in terms of the observations by think tanks, by a lot of media commentators, by independent authorities ... and a whole range of parliamentary committees ... that poverty is really a major challenge in the United Kingdom and not nearly enough is currently being done to address the challenges. On the other side, what I found in my discussions with ministers is basically a state of denial, the ministers who I met told me that things are going well, that they don't see any big problems, and they are happy with the ways in which their policies are playing out.[19]

Alston's remarks were met with disdain by the Conservative government of the time, who rebuked his claims by saying the report was "barely believable" and that "the UK is one of the happiest places in the world to live".[20] The government refused to acknowledge the effects of their own policies and went on the defence. If a UN special rapporteur is disbelieved, and dismissed, what does this say about the likelihood of government believing in women and their families' experiences of poverty and debt? This question speaks volumes of the past Tory and Liberal Democrat coalition government who designed austerity and allowed it to run riot in their neoliberal reshaping of the country as an "elite-driven, capital-centric, shrunken welfare state project".[21] Yet austerity was "unavoidable" according to George Osborne's infamous emergency budget speech made in June 2010:

> This Budget is needed to deal with our country's debts. This Budget is needed to give confidence to our economy. This is the unavoidable Budget . . .
>
> Our policy is to raise from the ruins of an economy built on debt a new, balanced economy where we save, invest and export . . .
>
> An economy where prosperity is shared among all sections of society and all parts of the country . . .
>
> Mr Deputy Speaker, let me now address the largest bill in government – the welfare bill.
>
> It is simply not possible to deal with a budget deficit of this size without undertaking lasting reform of welfare . . .
>
> We've had to relearn the virtue of financial prudence.[22]

Here the then chancellor emphasizes pragmatism and the moral imperative for the repayment of "our" country's debts as an act of virtuous caution that all should accept. Very much on show here is the political convention that driving down public debt is the responsible course of action. This is a narrative that is far from a Conservative one alone. From the outset of her tenure, Rachel Reeves, the Labour government chancellor, has established fiscal rules that prioritize debt falling as a proportion of the economy.[23] Akin to Thatcher's call to "balance the books", Reeves' approach frames reducing debts as the only responsible economic approach, regardless of what a lack of public expenditure might mean for people reliant on welfare and public services who are already scraping by.

Such attitudes are something that heterodox economists who challenge mainstream thinking are increasingly questioning. *The Deficit Myth* is perhaps the most lauded (and controversial) example. Stephanie Kelton's main thesis in the book is that calls for fiscal action on government debt are flawed given that deficit is a myth; it is in fact feasible for large deficits to run alongside the magical word, "growth". This is because a high degree of monetary sovereignty as a currency issuer means countries such as the UK can always pay the bills, "even the big ones".[24] Margaret Thatcher's famous espousal that government finances are constrained like those of a household is wrong, Kelton argues. Not only this, but "because we've been trained to believe, like each of us, the government must 'find the money' before it can spend, everyone becomes obsessed with the question: How are you going to pay for it?"[25] Former Prime Minister Theresa May's infamous words, that "there is no magic money tree", is a false provocation by this logic. The national debt that austerity was designed to reduce is a myth, a work of falsification, according to Kelton. Fiscal disciplining of such households in England is, nevertheless, still in vogue according to the 2025 Spring Statement. Rachel Reeves stands accused of wearing "the mask of tough decisions, but on a stage built on myths".[26]

Withstanding these compelling arguments about the deficit myth, our own book is not intended as a deep dive into the minefield of financial theory and debate. *Debt Trap Nation* is focused instead on the human costs of the deficit reduction programme that austerity unleashed, and that are *irresponsibly* high. The obsessive thirst for "fixing" public debt as espoused by Osborne and others since disregards the debts borne by families in turning to market-based survival that is trapping them in housing precarity. It is crucial, as political economist Johnna Montgomerie argues, to consider how "household sector debt exists in relation to the national debt".[27] Several commentators in the early years of austerity pointed to the ocular failures of government, which only saw government debt as of concern, keeping out of sight the more significant problem of private debt.[28] What decision-makers and policy-makers refused to see and act on was the "mobility of debt" and its unevenly distributed burdens arising from private debt transformed into public debt, and governmental debt transmitted into personal debt.[29] Economist Paul Krugman explains the logic behind his hypothesis that household debt in Britain would rise in response to austerity:

> Why? Because the only way the economy can avoid taking a hit from government cuts is if private spending rises to fill the gap – and although you rarely hear the austerians admitting this, the only way that can happen is if people take on more debt. So we have the spectacle of a government that inveighs against the evils of debt pinning all its hopes on an assumption that over-indebted households will dig their hole even deeper.[30]

What transpired was that predicted. The vast and multifaceted reductions in welfare provision have left increasing numbers of families vulnerable to debt in a range of ways: from rent and bill arrears, to relying on payday loans to bridge gaps in earnings. This could be thought of as the "scalar dumping" of risk, debts and deficits under austerity by central government to impoverished citizens and their respective local authorities.[31] Although debt among low-income households is not necessarily a new trend, this group has encountered the greatest growth in unsecured debt-to-income ratio under austerity in Britain, much of which is for everyday essentials.[32] The roll-back of the welfare state has had a direct impact on problem debt with family homelessness a telling outcome. For the most financially vulnerable then, the debt trap is a form of market dependence and market-based power that is difficult to get away from in our austere, neoliberalized and financialized society.

Unhoming tendencies of the debt trap

At its centre, the debt trap is a process of unhoming: an eroding and erasure of home. This unhoming is intimately tied to England's political and economic trajectory and lays the foundations for the debt trap's existence. Mothers are, again, disproportionately impacted by unhoming given their normative responsibilization in this role to provide a home to mother from and offer a sense of homeliness to their children. In Victorian England this gendered norm was especially pronounced as women were expected to be the domesticated, sacrificial and virtuous "Angel of the House". While societal attitudes have clearly evolved, typically women are still at the forefront of homemaking practices and responsibilities, and being a mother still conjures up ideals of mothering (e.g. self-sacrifice) that women variously identify with or not. Problem debt, domestic abuse and homelessness erode women's capacity to mother "at home" both emotionally and in practical terms.

This is because, at the time of writing, there are 80,532 households with dependent children living in temporary accommodation, a rise of 15.7 per cent in a year and a population representing 64 per cent of all households in temporary accommodation.[33] In comparison to single-person households, the numbers of households with dependent children are part of a much steeper upward trajectory of numbers since the austerity era began in 2010.[34]

The geographical concentration of households living in temporary accommodation are marked in England's major cities: London, Manchester and Birmingham.[35] Households where the lead homelessness applicant is White make up the highest percentage share in temporary accommodation in both London and the rest of the country. This insight, however, does not tell the full story of the racialized aspects of homelessness. According to government figures, there are a disproportionate number of Black and other ethnic group households in temporary accommodation in comparison to their overall population size in both London and the rest of England.[36]

Families' encounters of the unhoming effects of the debt trap are also felt through the multiple moves that they are often forced to make, at speed, between temporary accommodations locally, across administrative boundaries or across the country. Mothers face being deemed "intentionally homeless" if they do not agree to these forced migrations, despite losses of community, kin and friendship networks, employment and the stability of their children's education. Data published by the Office of the Children's Commissioner for England show that there is a direct correlation between the amount a child moves accommodation and lower GCSE pass rates.[37] Put otherwise, educational inequality is writ large through the denial of a secure home and life on the move. A generation of children risk being trapped in poverty through poor educational prospects as a direct result of state failings to tackle the housing crisis and child poverty. And there is growing evidence of children being moved far away from their schools and lifeworlds as local authorities, particularly in London, try to source cheaper accommodation elsewhere. More than £140 million is being spent by London councils and their housing providers to relocate households out of the capital,[38] including as far away as Liverpool.[39] At the time of writing, 31 per cent of households (36,360) in temporary accommodation are placed in a different local authority district from the one they had registered as homeless with, and 78.9 per cent of these out-of-district placements were from London authorities.[40] Homeless families are not allowed to dwell in the England of today, especially not in its high-cost cities, but rather are uprooted and dispersed through coercion not choice.

So how did we as a nation get to this point? It has been well documented that the introduction of the Right to Buy scheme in 1980, whereby council tenants were offered large discounts to purchase their homes, dramatically reduced council housing stock. In this scheme are some of the makings of a debt-trapped nation. Right to Buy stipulated that earnings from council house sales could not be used by local authorities to invest in new stock. Four decades after Right to Buy was introduced, local authorities are building less than 5 per cent of all housing in England and Wales.[41] The resulting social housing deficit is marked: since 1991 there has been an average annual net loss of 24,000 social homes in England.[42] A key outcome of this has been a mass transfer of people from social housing to the much more precarious private rented sector. There are now 1.4 million fewer households in social housing than in 1980; in the same period, the number of households living in the private rented sector has doubled.[43] White British households are less likely than most other ethnic groups to rent their home privately in England, and the private rented sector has the highest proportion of ethnic minorities compared to other tenures.[44] Increasing numbers of people have little choice but to live in housing that costs on average one-third of households' pre-tax earnings. Renters in the private sector spend a greater proportion of their incomes on rent than any other housing tenure.[45] Not only this, but one of the most likely groups to have low financial resilience – being in problem debt or having limited capacity to withstand financial shocks – are renters (47 per cent). Other groups include unemployed adults (48 per cent), adults with household income less than £15,000 (50 per cent) and adults from a Black ethnic group (44 per cent) or from multiple ethnic groups (39 per cent).[46]

The increasing role of high-cost, low-security private rented housing has fed directly into rising rates of family homelessness. Between 2013 and 2018 the number of working families evicted from private rented housing because of rent arrears or rent increases rose by 73 per cent.[47] In 2023, owing to a combination of unaffordability and insecurity, evictions from the private rented sector were at an eight-year high.[48] The loss of a private tenancy is the leading cause of homelessness in England, and it is people from Black and Mixed ethnic backgrounds that have some of the highest levels of homelessness. Black people are three and a half times as likely to experience this as White British people.[49] In other words, housing inequality, low finance resilience, and risks of homelessness are highly racialized. The reduced role of the state in housing provision laid the groundwork, therefore, for significant rises in family homelessness over the past four decades that further the political neglect of minoritized groups.

Political decision-making has shifted to largely benefit private interests over public ones. Nearly half (41 per cent) of homes sold under the Right to Buy scheme are now in the private market.[50] Conor O'Shea, policy and public affairs manager at Generation Rent, reflects that "it is no surprise that the haemorrhaging of homes from the social sector to the hands of private landlords has been a failure for those who actually live there".[51] Landlordism in England has been fuelled by credit, especially buy-to-let mortgages in the 1990s and 2000s, which supercharged the profit-seeking private rented sector that now houses 4.6 million (19 per cent of all) households in England.[52] Easy access to credit for landlords, based on rental yield rather than on borrowers' income, fuelled the private rented sector and the "rentier capitalism" we see today: the building up of monetized value for investors and owners through credit. There are clear racial dynamics to landlordism that reflect financial inequalities in England more broadly. In the English Private Landlord Survey 2021, 88 per cent of landlords identified as White, 4 per cent as Indian, 2 per cent as Black, 1 per cent as Pakistani or Bangladeshi, and the remaining 5 per cent as Other (with little difference in portfolio size). Landlords who identify as male (55 per cent) tend to own more rental properties than the 45 per cent of female landlords.[53]

Large-scale landlordism has rocketed since the 2008 global financial crisis. Private equity companies have been especially aggressive in their debt-based expansion of residential real estate portfolios, including the "parking" of money in cities such as London.[54] City Wire, an asset management company based in the capital, reports that: "Private equity firms are chomping at the bit to get their hands on residential real estate in the UK, as the country's housing shortage, the growing costs of being a private landlord, and the rising price of home ownership create a gap for investors to swoop in."[55]

In sum, governments have failed to protect the propertyless, allowing capital to eat up social housing without replenishing it, and letting landlords and private capital run amok. In the run-up to the July 2024 general election, Andy Burnham's message as mayor of Greater Manchester to Whitehall and Westminster was that the Right to Buy scheme should be suspended.[56] This plea was ignored in Labour's first Autumn Budget. Rather, the government announced reduced discounts for council house purchases: an intermediate measure to say the least. Since the Autumn Budget, however, in November 2024 the government announced a new consultation to put further conditions and limits on the scheme. Finally, it seems, there is some acknowledgement of the damage caused by this huge transfer of housing stock. Yet to dismantle the debt trap means more profound and radical change than tinkering around the edges; Right to Buy as one of the most disastrous policy prescriptions in the last 50 years needs to be abolished.

Fault at the debtor's door

For most of us, debt is, in one way or another, an omnipresent aspect of our lives. Having said this, there is a blatant disparity between the facilitative importance of credit in peoples' everyday lives and the harsh moral and personal judgements that are made about *certain* borrowing and borrowers. Despite the unavoidable reality of credit-taking, particularly among low-income households in austere times, fault is constructed to sit with the debtor. As Claer Barrett, consumer editor at the *Financial Times* frames it, "debt is one of the last taboos".[57]

People in England who take out mortgage loans are on the other hand generally not considered at fault or stigmatized; rather, they are considered to be making a logical financial decision. Their borrowing is in keeping with the idea of England as a "property-owning democracy" espoused by Thatcher and established through a mortgage-led accumulation regime.[58] Conversely, types of debt that are more common among low-income households, such as store credit and payday loans, are regularly associated with financial illiteracy and reckless behaviour. Citizens Advice believe these associations persist, even though this "isn't about people borrowing more than they can afford or not budgeting well enough to repay debts ... for many the sums just don't add up".[59] Not only this, but while "mortgage holidays" are possible for homeowners to temporarily reduce or pause their monthly mortgage payments, rarely is such flexibility afforded to renters facing arrears. Missing payments in the private rented sector are usually swiftly followed by eviction notices. This is despite the fact that for years, if not decades, tenants will have been working and making sacrifices to line landlords' pockets and boost their housing wealth with no accrued financial benefit for themselves and in increasingly dire housing conditions. As barrister Nick Bano explains, "rent extraction and land value speculation are perhaps the closest thing that Britain has to a national industry... What is it that makes housing in Britain such a reliable and attractive investment? The answer is ratcheting rents."[60]

In our research, while individuals' debts, even rent arrears, are generally small and negligible in pure financial terms, they are having a huge and disproportionate negative impact on mothers and their children's lives. Returning to Graeber,[61] we can see how families' suffering is justified as a "matter of impersonal arithmetic – and by doing so, to justify things that would otherwise seem outrageous or obscene". That the debts such as Evie's are *so small* speaks strongly to this sentiment. As we argue later, this brutal approach extends to social housing allocation in England and the discrimination faced by indebted households in these "sorting" processes. In response to a public talk we gave, the director of The Magpie Project, Jane Williams, wrote to us to say: "The basic notion of looking at these families in terms of financial risk as tenants rather than families at risk who need housing is quite astounding and I had not clocked it before." Jane's observation goes to the heart of what is wrong, what is rotten, in the way that families are viewed and treated as financial liabilities.

The possibility of compassion for those experiencing housing-related debt is undermined too by a policy discourse that codifies and generalizes debt as "unacceptable behaviour". "Stigma is purposely crafted as a strategy of government", argues Tyler.[62] Debt and its repayment are framed as more than financial, embroiled in personal obligation that must be behaviourally mustered and ultimately honoured to deserve housing. This framing obscures the political responsibility for that very debt. Again, Graeber's insights are revealing here: "If history shows anything, it is that there's no better way to justify relations founded on violence, to make such relations seem moral, than by reframing them in the language of debt – above all, because it immediately makes it seem that it's the victim who's doing something wrong."[63]

English society is bound up in the idea that the debt trap is one that households have indulgently, or recklessly, fallen into because of some sort of personal failure. There persists a moral fixation on debt as self-indulgent in the national psyche. Debts that must be honoured or else the borrower is tarnished with being "delinquent". The "solution" to debt delinquency is to hide behind a smokescreen of responsibilization under neoliberalism. The psychology academic Carl Walker explains relatedly how the onus on personal debt management in national policy formulation, and the idea that problem debt is in a household's control to avoid, essentially obscures the macroeconomic reasons for that debt in favour of claiming financial incompetence.[64] Such an approach means that the complex and structural reasons for that debt are concealed, and government guilt absolved, in favour of a political ideology that emphasizes blaming individual culpability. This is politically convenient; it protects the neoliberal status quo. Individual and household obligations, in both financial and moral guises, are impressed upon to naturalize the consequences of not delivering on that obligation. This obligation then puts pressures, financially and emotionally, on the debtor, as a trained neoliberal subject, to repay. Such fear, shame and stigma coalesce to compel borrowers to take responsibility for their debts (such as missing meals, as Evie did), whatever the consequences.

Considering these harms and sacrifices, *Debt Trap Nation* joins a growing chorus of feminist scholars studying and pushing back on debt in what the authors of *A Feminist Reading of Debt* call a "political move against guilt".[65] This political move involves taking debt "out of the closet": "Taking it out of the closet means *making it visible and situating it as a common problem*, de-individualizing it. Because taking debt out of the closet involves challenging its power to shame and guilt and its power to function as a 'private issue,' which we can only face by managing our accounts alone."[66]

A Feminist Reading of Debt contends, therefore, that there is an urgency to "de-privatize" debt, "give it a body, a voice, and a territory".[67] Our own book is part of this endeavour to reject the simple, the cold, the impersonal, in favour of bringing the debt trap into complex, compassionate and personal view. Such an approach enables us to think more about the Marxist feminist call to re-evaluate "who owes what to whom?"[68] What about the huge debt that society owes women and mothers? Social reproductive burdens on women have been heightened by deficient public services under austerity. Not only this, but austerity in England has externalized the costs of social reproduction onto families who are getting into problem debt in response. As the philosopher Nancy Fraser elaborates, "reducing the 'social wage' by dismantling public provision, it entangles the bulk of the non-propertied populations in the tentacles of debt".[69]

Women's monetary debt is thus linked to state public debt. Life under austerity means the repayment of this state public debt is prioritized to the detriment of honouring the social contract with its citizens. In other words, when national debts are repaid, money is lost from key services including housing, healthcare, social protection and so on. Activist Silvia Federici explains in turn that, as "the lending-debt machine becomes the main means of reproduction, a new class relation is produced where the exploiters are more hidden, more removed, and the mechanisms of exploitation are far more individualized and guilt producing".[70] Escaping and abolishing the debt trap is, we contend, a counterhegemonic project tied to structural change and the making tangible of exploitation. It is also a political project of inversion in which neoliberal patriarchal inscriptions of who is creditor and who is debtor are questioned and reversed.

Embodying the trap, embodying harm

So far, we have established that the debt trap is one that is difficult or impossible to avoid. Not only this, but it is bound up in an ideology-fuelled blame game that works against the well-being of homeless families in England today. The material deprivation as well as emotional exhaustion of living with debt are encapsulated in families' experiences of homelessness and living in temporary accommodation. Long-term unsecured debt, and residing in temporary accommodation, are both, unsurprisingly, negative for people's physical and mental health.[71] Impacts can be wide-ranging, from poor quality sleep and insomnia, financial melancholia, depression and anxiety, to the attritional physical and mental effects of sacrificing food or heating to repay debts. As we have explained, the debt trap is not just an economic binding, it is an ideological one. Given the weight put on individual responsibility in neoliberal doctrine, guilt and shame among debtors can be conceived of as emotional responses generated by the transgression of normative value systems. In this sense the "coercive quality of debt relations is often latent",[72] meaning that the feminist goal of bringing the violence of debt "out of the closet" is especially prescient.

A focus on embodying the debt trap serves as a political act by making tangible what is at stake: people's short and longer-term health, well-being and happiness. Embodiment in feminist theory, as we embrace it, aids us in better understanding not only the fleshly material but also the emotional and affective dimensions of debt and homelessness as contextually situated in time and space. Harm and trauma are embodied in the sense that they are real, sensory and physical.[73] A key goal of the book, then, is to foreground homeless single mothers' embodied experiences of how the debt trap as an architecture of harm is being produced and, with these grounded expert knowledges, how the debt trap can be dismantled.

Debt as a driver and outcome of housing precarity looms large in women's accounts of the debt trap we have listened to and learned from. What it means and feels to navigate it can be found in every corner of England and expressed in novel forms. In May 2023 we visited the Brighton Fringe and watched a show called "Home: The Intimacy of Debt and Inequality". The show's promotional material promised audiences a journey through the home in which "aerial acrobats scale sky-high towers of debt and contort around the housing ladder".[74] The performance delivered. We watched an academic research project on asset-based inequality in the UK by Mareike Beck turned into an eight-act show that took the audience into the embodied life of debt. The performers (including Beck herself) balanced and juggled debt, twisted and turned to make ends meet, span out of control, and were found "on the ropes" risking eviction because of the privileging of financial gain for the investment "fat cats".[75]

The use of performance art to show the meeting of the body with the politics and economics of home and debt has some echoes with Gustav Peebles' anthropological writing. He identifies credit and debt as foregrounding the visceral everyday connections between the body of the individual and that of the nation.[76] Under austerity, the cutting of national debts has been wielded against the already vulnerable, their embodied lives and rights to home cut down in the name of fiscal responsibility. Austerity, born out of the current-day devotion to a macroeconomy characterized by neoliberalism and market fundamentalism is "structurally pathogenic" in its negative impacts on peoples' health.[77] The debt trap is cut from the same cloth. That the debt trap goes hand in hand with family homelessness only strengthens the legitimacy of this assertion. Moreover, the penalties of the trap are gendered; act seven of the acrobatic show in Brighton was aptly titled: "Who calculates, manages and cares for all that debt? The gendered division of labour. But what if we stopped to care?" This returns us importantly to the feminist questioning of who owes what to who in society today.

Imprisoned in debt

Many of the women we spoke to used the word "prison" to describe temporary accommodation. Across England, from Birmingham, to London, to Liverpool, "prison" or "prison-like" are labels used by families talking to the press about their experiences in temporary accommodation.[78] As we have mentioned, families are typically pushed into homelessness and temporary accommodation because of rent arrears amassed in the private rented sector and/or through domestic abuse. On the latter front, for some women who experienced domestic abuse, the sense of being a prisoner was not new. Preceding their entry into temporary accommodation, women's descriptions of their past homes read more like cages than the havens traditionally associated with domestic life (a discourse that was especially strong in nineteenth-century England).[79] This sense arises because domestic abuse is, in fact, a "liberty crime"; perpetrators try to entrap victims and undermine their social support and autonomy.[80] As feminist geographer Rachel Pain elaborates, chronic trauma is often the consequence of repeated exposure to such violence; physical, psychological, material, and social isolation can then manifest and contribute to (fears of) limited prospects to escape.[81] Given that freedom arises from the capabilities to choose what an individual has reason to value, domestic abuse victims can feel, and be, trapped in place by the (perceived) untenability of leaving to secure safety and freedom.

This can be a matter of life and death. Experiences of economic abuse, for example, can drive arrears and debt, which can make it harder to leave. Research by the charity Surviving Economic Abuse revealed that nearly a quarter of women in the UK who have suffered domestic abuse were prevented from leaving a dangerous partner because of economic coercion and control.[82] Nearly one million women are trapped in a dangerous relationship because of economic abuse. Clearly there are, as StepChange Debt Charity and Gingerbread explain, "limited options for survivors of economic abuse left with coerced debt from an abusive relationship" given that "one legacy of abuse for many single parents is serious problem debt".[83]

As we go on to further evidence, mothers are being trapped in abusive relationships by their perpetrator, by debt and by the prospect of prolonged homelessness if they do leave. Upon becoming homeless in a statutory sense, they are put in temporary accommodation under a sentence of unknown duration before (potentially) being placed in social housing. Barry Schwartz, a psychologist, wrote in the 1970s that to be kept waiting, "especially to be kept waiting an unusually long time, is to be the subject of an assertion that one's own time (and therefore, one's social worth) is less valuable than the time and worth of the one who imposes the wait".[84] Homeless families in England are residing in a protracted state of limbo, waiting. While the most common length of time for single households to stay in temporary accommodation is fewer than six months, households with children are spending two to five years there.[85]

Mothers and their children across England, and particularly its major cities, are imprisoned bodies outside of prison and detention spaces but cramped in what geographers call "quasi-carceral" spaces that can resemble formal sites of confinement.[86] Temporary accommodation is one such space, where homeless families' lives can become trapped because of debt and lengthy waiting lists. This is the latest iteration in England's long history of punishing debtors and curtailing their freedoms. In the eighteenth and nineteenth centuries, debtors' prisons were used to house tens of thousands who owed creditors for (often small) unpaid debts.[87] Here, "moral regeneration" was the order of the day so that debtors would be reformed, grasping their obligations to repay through the denial of "pleasures" and rejection of loose morals.[88] Debt remains, today, a morally legitimizing technology of guilt and control that can curtail people's freedoms in the present and future. Temporary accommodation has become, we argue, the debtors' prison of the twenty-first century.

"Temporary" spaces of extraction

Ruth Wilson-Gilmore, an American prison abolitionist and geographer, argues that prisons are "primed for extractive activity to unfold".[89] What she means by this is that the expansion of prison populations in the United States since the 1980s, especially targeting and incarcerating people of colour, has been pursued for revenue generation and private profit. We see some parallels with growing numbers of families, again disproportionately populated by Black and Mixed ethnic backgrounds in England who are trapped in temporary accommodation. Private profit is maximized not only via the mandated repayment of loans and their interest by households but also through the furnishing of private profit for temporary accommodation owners and brokers paid for through ever-dwindling local authority funds. The impact of state failings to invest in enough social housing, and to control escalating rents in the private rented sector, have left local authorities in England spending colossal sums of public money on temporary accommodation. Local authorities and housing associations procure temporary accommodation through private sector leasing to meet their statutory duty to offer it for homeless households. With this, a lucrative temporary accommodation market has emerged in England. In London alone, £4 million is being spent *per day* on temporary accommodation.[90] In response to a 2025 investigation by *Inside Housing* and *i Paper* on the economics of temporary accommodation, Rick Henderson, chief executive of Homeless Link, asserts: "We need to break this cycle of funding temporary solutions, which is bad for the public purse, and, more importantly, bad for the individual people and families who are stuck in it."[91]

As Evie herself reflected in the opening pages of this book, the bad economics of it make no sense. Shelter have pointed out in the frankest of terms that temporary accommodation providers are essentially "cashing in". The charity's research on the sector shows that it is the private providers who do not own temporary accommodation properties but instead work as brokers between local authorities and private investors, that are earning the most profit. These profits arise from the margin between the guaranteed rents to investors and the nightly rates they charge local authorities.[92] The entry of brokers into the marketplace means that local authorities are left spending more on high, often nightly, rates or booking budget hotels, such as Travelodge and Premier Inn chains. There is also growing evidence of family homes, particularly in London, being bought by landlords with the explicit goal of turning them into HMOs (houses in multiple occupation) as temporary accommodation becomes increasingly lucrative. For the JRF,

> This represents a dysfunctional situation, where it is far more lucrative for a landlord to provide short-term accommodation than it is to provide a decent, long-term home, and where landlords are not only capitalising on the homelessness crisis, but are also prolonging it by reducing the supply of homes that homeless families could otherwise move into.[93]

In November 2024, the cross-party Housing, Communities and Local Government Committee held its first evidence session concerning children living in temporary accommodation and evidence was given that substantiated this view too. Laura Neilson, chief executive of the Shared Health Foundation, testified:

> Local landlords are switching accommodation from social [or] private rent into temporary accommodation, because they can get higher payments from the council ... So they'll evict a family from their property, change it into temporary accommodation and move another family into that property for higher rent. And we're seeing that reasonably often.[94]

Arguably, this market emergence and profit-seeking set of marketplace behaviours represent what Naomi Klein calls "disaster capitalism", when the response to a disaster or emergency opens up a conducive and opportunistic environment for private profit and the further entrenchment of socio-economic inequality.[95] Temporary accommodation providers are, in this light, not only financially benefitting from a failing state but also making these profits by draining the "public purse". Families' detriment is a source of profit for private landlords and investors in temporary accommodation as they extract surplus economic value from the state and homeless people trying to survive in a failing state. There is no incentive to rock the status quo that temporary accommodation is anything but temporary. They are not just beneficiaries but also agents in the assetization and financialization of housing that is partly responsible for the family homelessness crisis. In *Vulture Capitalism*, journalist Grace Blakeley makes the aligned argument that modern crises are the *intended* result of the capitalism system. Connecting to our own focus, this would mean, for example, that failing to build enough social housing is not a failure in the eyes of the private housebuilding industry.[96] Not only have they got their claws into remaining development land for newbuilds but they also received state support through schemes such as Help to Buy, which was introduced in 2013 to extract profit.[97]

The result is that councils are spending more than £2 billion on temporary accommodation in a single year, and many are sounding the alarm of potential bankruptcy because of these costs. New Members of Parliament taking office after the July 2024 general election were greeted with a "quick read" brief on why local authorities are going bankrupt. Austerity has left local councils under severe financial strain at a time of intensifying pressures to fulfil their statutory duties to secure a roof for the increasing numbers of homeless households. The District Councils' Network hosted 158 councils in autumn 2023 at an emergency summit over rising temporary accommodation costs and concerns that many councils were on the brink of insolvency. Council leader Stephen Holt of Eastbourne Borough Council described the situation as a "national crisis" and that expenditure for temporary accommodation accounted for 49 pence for every £1 of council tax collected.[98] This worrying financial outlook is exacerbated by a 2011 decision made by central government to cap the amount of money local authorities can claim from them for temporary accommodation costs. This cap remains and it is left to local authorities across England to pay for the shortfall in the hundreds of millions.

In July 2024, the new Deputy Prime Minister Angela Rayner acknowledged in her speech at a Local Government Association event that the situation was dire, "As council leaders, one of the biggest pressures you face is the issue of homelessness. You're stuck in a doom loop with soaring temporary accommodation costs, crippling council budgets preventing you from fixing the long-term problems."[99]

As the phrase "stuck in a doom loop" suggests, the debt trap looms large in Rayner's appraisal of the costs of temporary accommodation to local authorities unable to balance their books. These wildly high costs mean local authorities are also struggling to find the budget to build new social housing stock. A month ahead of the July 2024 election, The Local Government Association published its Local Government White Paper. In it, the association set out the "biggest challenges" local government faced, one of them being, not unsurprisingly, the record-breaking numbers of homeless families and children.[100]

Not at home in a failing state

Debt Trap Nation aims to show how it is not just the housing market but a whole raft of connected challenges that need to be thought about differently to meet families' needs now and in the future. A failing state is not a failure for all, namely private and corporate interests that are profiting from the housing emergency England faces. Maybe this is what the government of the time meant in saying to Philip Alston that they were "happy" with how their policies were playing out? It's not just a question of how the debt trap was set but also a question of what vested interests are there in keeping it. To be "not at home" in a failing state is to be on the receiving end of politics where power lies in the hands of a political system in which the economic and political elite cooperate for their mutual benefit. This is state capitalism writ large: one in which banks are bailed out and citizens are turfed out. In the chapters that follow we open up the debt trap further through the lives of mothers and their children on the front line of the here-and-now scandal that is family homelessness.

CHRISTINE

Life Expert at the All-Party Parliamentary Group for Households in Temporary Accommodation, 10 October 2023

The Debt Trap

I am here today to tell you about my lived experience of homelessness and debt.

A Bit of Background

I was working in the primary school my children attended. My son was around six years old and in Year 1. My daughter was around five years old and in reception class.

Domestic Violence

In 2009 I left the marital home with my two children as I feared for our safety. The key workers at the refuge insisted on using the term Domestic Violence – two words I would soon come to realize encapsulated the life I had been living. We arrived at the refuge with just one suitcase and remained there for 18 months waiting to be housed and trying to rebuild our lives.

School

Initially, when we moved to the refuge, I left my job and enrolled the children into a primary school closer to where we were staying, but we were all very unhappy. With the help and support of our previous headteacher, I returned to my job (part-time) and took the children back to the one place that would be familiar and stable for them.

Homeless and in Debt

Shock #1

The tenancy was in his name only.

He had previously convinced me that only one signature was required for a married couple on a Tenancy. I had been deceived.

Shock #2

I now had a £13,000 debt solely in my name.

During our marriage I had been coerced into taking out various bank loans (as he was not eligible) to cover shortfalls in rent, bills and daily living costs. He continuously promised he would pay it off when he found a job – he never worked!

Shock #3

I applied for Child Maintenance and the notification returned surmised that the amount he had to pay to support his children was zero pounds.

My Finances

- Every time I moved (refuge/temp/perm) I would be reassessed for benefits (Housing Benefit, Council Tax, Tax Credits, etc.). The calculations were very complex and despite my transparency, by the time I reached permanent accommodation I ended up in significant rent arrears and had to set up a repayment plan.
- I continued with my loan repayments (from £13,000 debt).
- I had to buy school uniforms, school shoes, PE kits, coats, bags . . .
- I paid for a monthly Travelcard as we commuted to work/school daily by bus and tube – I was not eligible for Free School Meals for the children.
- I had moving expenses (refuge/temp/perm accomm).
- And, for our permanent accommodation I had to purchase white goods, furniture and flooring.

This was all in addition to covering rent, utility bills, food bills, dentist and optician visits (for myself), school clubs, school trips, school events . . .

Individual Voluntary Arrangement

After years of "robbing Peter to pay Paul"[101] (as my late mother would say) – credit cards, loans, hire-purchase and catalogue credit, in 2020 I took out an IVA

[Individual Voluntary Arrangement][102] to try and put an end to my debts. Then, in 2021 I was unexpectedly made redundant and used the majority of my redundancy payout to honour my debts under the IVA.

In Conclusion

In 2022 I was finally given a lifetime tenancy with the local council.

Also in 2022, I received my certificate of completion for the IVA but this will remain on my credit file until September 2028!

And, the generational trauma of debt and poverty continues.

- My son is now 20 years of age and working in a minimum-wage paid job.
- My daughter is 19 years of age and in her second year of university (with a student loan).

Thank you for listening.

*

YOU
TURN
ON
SURVIVAL
MODE

3

Indebted (after) lives of domestic abuse

Irhaa picked up the Pritt stick and applied some glue to the back of the paper cut-out. Turning it over and pressing it firmly against the rolled-out collage paper, she looked back from the sheet. Affixed to the timeline of her life was now an image of a glass milk bottle and cup filled with black milk. "He was just one of those people, if he said, 'the milk's black' and you'd be like 'are you daft? It's white', he would start an argument." Irhaa was talking about Auraq, her husband and father to their four boys. His emotional manipulation and distortion of reality – gaslighting – had lasted 13 years. We first met Irhaa in May 2022 at a baby bank that also provides holistic care for families who are homeless or at risk of homelessness in Greater Manchester.[1] We sat together in an office there, a small room with bright blue walls and a frosted window. On the sill sat a tissue box adorned with the affirmative mantra "Thrive".

Standing up from our swivel chairs, Irhaa traced her biography on the "journey map" we were creating. This was a visual representation of her journey through and beyond the times of abuse perpetrated by both Auraq and his mother.[2] The collage paper held down with a potted cactus on one edge and a stapler on the other, Irhaa wrote on each of the glued-down houses – each representing a house she had lived in – what it was like, the dates she lived there and the financial circumstances she faced in each.

After moving from her British Pakistani parents' home in northwest England in the mid-2000s, Irhaa began living with her newly-wed husband in his family home. It is on this glued-down house that she had impressed the image of black milk and made some annotations:

No choices
No control
Controlled
Emotionally + physically abused
Cheated on
Slavery
Broken nose, bruised eye

Irhaa, now in her thirties, was responsible for raising her boys and acting as full-time carer for her disabled mother-in-law who lived with them. At the start of her marriage, Auraq started to play mind games with her. Auraq's coercive and controlling behaviour included economic abuse. Surviving Economic Abuse notes that this is common in the context of intimate partner violence: it "involves the control of a partner or ex-partner's money and finances, as well as the things that money can buy".[3] Irhaa was granted very little access to money and her Carer's Allowance was kept entirely by Auraq. She describes the around-the-clock demands from her husband and emotionally abusive mother-in-law as "slavery". Trying to build a future for herself, she pleaded with him, initially without success, to be allowed to study at a local university. "So then I said to him, 'Look, I'm gonna get a student loan and I'll help you pay your debt off' . . . this was my negotiation with him." Easing her husband's existing debt by taking on more, in her name, was seemingly Irhaa's only route to building a life for herself.

Irhaa attended just six classes before the first Covid-19 lockdown arrived in March 2020. "I was having the time of my life and then the pandemic hit, and we had to stay at home." Unable to combine online study with family responsibilities, as school closures took hold and the demands of unpaid labour heaped on, she reluctantly quit the course. Like so many other women who were enduring domestic abuse prior to the pandemic, the physical violence worsened. She was trapped not just by the lockdown but also by her lack of financial autonomy, which Auraq had engineered. Frequent thoughts of leaving were painfully quashed in her mind, "putting up" with the violence was felt to be the only realistic option. Again and again, she anguished about the prospect of leaving, "How am I going to do it with the four kids financially?" The economic violence, two-child benefit cap and other intersecting gender inequalities that entrenched her economic dependency on Auraq curtailed her choices and ability to access safety.

Depicted as a "shadow pandemic", domestic abuse victims lived at increased risk from perpetrators and became further isolated as in-person service provision stopped.[4] It is widely considered that violence by current partners as well as by other family members increased during the lockdown periods. Researchers analysing Greater London data, for example, found that violence by current partners increased by 8 per cent and violence by family members as much as 17 per cent.[5] But the heightened dangers across 2020 and 2021 did not arise in a vacuum. Domestic abuse is a systemic problem that consecutive governments have failed to address through lack of support and investment in services to protect women. Instead, the domestic abuse sector and the meeting of women's needs has seen drastic cuts to funding as part of the UK's programme of austerity. Legal aid is now in tatters, and refuges either lack long-term sustainable funding or have been closed.[6] Women's access to safe spaces outside of the family home has been restricted rather than enabled. Such is the long-running harm of austerity that Oxfam International has characterized the macroeconomic policy choice taken by governments, around the world, as gender-based violence:

> Austerity is not just a gendered policy; it is also a gendered process in its "everydayness" – the way it permeates the daily lives of women specifically: in their incomes, their care responsibilities, their ability to access services as essential as health, water and transportation, and in their overall safety and freedom from physical violence in the home, at work and on the street.[7]

For many working on women's rights and gender equality, including socio-legal scholars Jane Krishnadas and Sophia Taya, domestic abuse is a tool of patriarchal oppression in which the "home is not, and has never been, a place of safety".[8] That women's basic needs have not been valued enough to be funded by the state is case in point they argue. In these circumstances, the charity Women's Aid urges that the "pandemic cannot be used to excuse the deficiencies that were already present prior to the pandemic".[9]

For Irhaa, the mobility restrictions at the height of the first Covid-19 lockdown combined with the drying up of Auraq's taxi driving meant he was home far more. Unable to escape for respite to her parents' house, Irhaa was trapped and the violence intensified. The Covid-19 Inquiry held in late 2023 was told that domestic abuse victims died during the lockdowns because of a lack of gender diversity among decision-makers in government and the "macho" culture that pervaded Downing Street. "Not only were there numerous examples of women being ignored, excluded, not listened to or talked over. It was also clear that the female perspective was being missed in advice and decision-making", revealed the then Deputy Cabinet Secretary Helen MacNamara.[10]

Misogyny, like austerity, kills. It is not only that misogyny and gender inequality lie at the very root of domestic abuse but also that misogyny emerges from and is perpetrated by decision-makers in government. The afterthought status of women such as Irhaa suffering domestic abuse during lockdown is an apt example. Early in the pandemic, this neglect was raised by Dame Vera Baird DBE QC, Victims' Commissioner for England and Wales, who put a question to the House of Commons as to why the increase of domestic abuse was a surprise for the government:

> It is very much harder to escape when you are compelled to be in lockdown with your perpetrator. What is in urgent need of rectification is the fact that the Government did not see this coming. In every other kind of crisis, there has been a similar development . . . it was obvious that there was going to be this epidemic within the pandemic.[11]

In her oral evidence, Baird noted the need for cash to support services struggling with increased demand and refuges being full. The very same month that the House of Commons listened to her criticisms of the lack of planning and domestic abuse "dropping through the silo" of any interministerial coordination, police were called to Irhaa and Auraq's house. Auraq had repeatedly punched Irhaa in the face leaving her with a broken nose and bruising to the eye. With the support of her siblings, she left the marital home with her children. Domestic abuse had led to family homelessness. Lockdown beckoned in a single hotel room for five weeks before a series of stays in other temporary accommodation. To make matters worse, council tax arrears and credit card loans sunk Irhaa into greater debt during this time.[12]

Irhaa is not alone in debt trap England – 43 per cent of the 72 respondents in a 2019 Women's Aid survey reported that they were in debt because of domestic abuse. The survey also found that of the women who had left their abusive partner, many were left homeless and almost one-third of them had turned to credit to survive. As a result, the charity concluded that "many survivors find themselves in debt, which can limit the choices available to them and create a barrier to moving forward in the future".[13] A 2020 survey with 360 victims in the UK during the Covid-19 pandemic by Surviving Economic Abuse found that eight out of ten women (79 per cent) reported that the perpetrator had attempted to control their finances during the pandemic, and that 60 per cent of economic abuse victims were coerced into debt.[14] Coerced debt, as Christine outlined in "Shock #3" of her testimony preceding this chapter, is debt generated through financial transactions that the victim is told to make – or is aware of the abuser making in their name. For London-based Christine, a White woman in her early fifties, this had taken the form of being coerced by her then partner into making bank loans. These consisted of £13,000 taken out in her sole name to repay rental arrears and buy essentials. Such coercion comes about in a context where there could be negative consequences for not complying. The Surviving Economic Abuse survey also discovered that one in five victims of economic violence were in rent or mortgage arrears since the beginning of the pandemic, compared to 14 per cent before the start of the outbreak. Since the peak of the Covid-19 pandemic, the issue of problem debt has not gone away. *The Guardian* has reported on domestic abuse victims in the UK left with "debt mountains" by abusive partners, also noting how these financial aspects are "poorly understood and can leave lives in ruins".[15]

In this chapter we start and finish with Irhaa's story to reveal both how domestic abuse is feeding the debt trap and how the debt trap is feeding domestic abuse. Through the pages that follow, we draw on the experiences of Irhaa, Christine, Casho, Jade and Zofia to show how domestic abuse, debt and family homelessness are close bedfellows. Patriarchal power and violence are rife, in both women's intimate relationships with men and their encounters with a failing state.

Controlled

In our regular visits to the baby bank where we met Irhaa and other research participants, the ongoing reality of domestic abuse was materially evident in a set of posters on the back of the bathroom door (Figure 3.1). When we first visited in May 2022, the posters were pristine and the takeaway contact information tabs hanging down were intact. Subsequent trips to the bathroom were a visceral reminder of the ongoing failures of government to prevent domestic abuse. By our third visit over a year later, nine tabs were gone. These were not the original sheets we had first clocked. They were fresh ones added to the same door, but now in alternate positions. The takeaway information was for the freephone Greater Manchester Domestic Abuse Helpline, a confidential source of support and advice to victims. With professionally trained staff, they can discuss legal options, safety planning and housing issues as well as access and referral to refuges across the UK. The helpline also provides emotional support to victims, "many of who[m] are taking a huge step by calling us in the first place".[16] As Irhaa's story echoes, both living with violence and thinking prospectively about leaving is huge in emotional and financial terms and requires dedicated external support.

Irhaa was a British citizen, but for other women without British citizenship or settled status, the options can be even more limited. An intersectional approach to understanding England as a debt-trapped nation is crucial to understanding its negative impacts on those who are already some of the most vulnerable in society. This need is crystalized in Casho's experiences. In the baby bank, Casho, in her mid-thirties, sat down gingerly on the office chair. She seemed nervous. But after a few minutes of chit-chat she relaxed and eased back into the seat. Casho began to open up, about the decade-long domestic abuse she experienced and the specific challenges she faced given her insecure immigration status. Born in Somalia, as a young adult Casho moved to Scandinavia with her sister. There she met her future husband, a British man who she moved to the UK with in the 2010s. Going on to have four children with Aaden, they lived together on the eighth floor of a tall block of council flats. The lift rarely worked, it was a "nightmare" with the pram, and Casho's eldest child complained regularly, "I will sleep on here, on the ground floor, I'm not walking up again!" Her husband reassured her that he was rebidding for more appropriate accommodation, but their move never materialized.

Figure 3.1 Domestic abuse poster at a baby bank in Greater Manchester

Source: Photo by K. Brickell, October 2023.

Casho had little control over their household finances. Aaden only provided her with money to buy essentials. On one occasion without telling her, he went on an overseas trip and took all the debit cards. She was left without money to even buy food. Surviving Economic Abuse explains how economic abuse tends to take three forms: restriction, exploitation and sabotage.[17] In this case, Aaden was heavily restricting Casho and their children to the point of hunger. Not only was her access to money and finances controlled but access to essentials – in this case food – was denied. This also goes for transportation. When Casho was eight months pregnant Aaden refused to give her a lift in the family's car to the hospital for a check-up appointment: "You think I'm losing sleep *for you?*" Aaden chastised. "So I asked for money to take a taxi, he said 'walk'." The walk was over two hours, there and back. At home, Aaden habitually followed Casho to the toilet, standing at the door waiting.

The financial control was combined with emotional abuse and he threatened to report her to the authorities for mistreating their children. The claim was entirely false. Aaden also taunted her with the risk of homelessness, "'leave, this is my house' he would say".

With no family in England and no friends close by, she felt painfully isolated and alone, "I didn't have anyone to talk to". To avoid being in the flat, after dropping her children off at school, Casho filled the day roaming the streets, "I just walked around doing nothing, tired, not eating anything, crying". Desperate for help she reached out to her children's primary school. They supported her to contact social services, but as there were deemed to be no specific issues with her children's safety or school attendance nothing was formally taken forwards. Due to her insecure immigration status, a key potential means to access public funds from her local authority via Section 17 of the Children Act 1989 would, therefore, not be available if she left Aaden. In social services' limited intervention, Casho was advised to stay with her abusive husband until she could secure Indefinite Leave to Remain. "'You need to go back' they told me. I said, 'I'm not going back'. They replied, 'you have to . . . you're not allowed a house'". Casho was advised that she would have no recourse to public funds (NRPF) (e.g. access to Universal Credit or housing) if she left Aaden.[18]

The Domestic Abuse Commissioner for England and Wales, Nicole Jacobs, has raised this spectre: of migrant victims without secure immigration status "shut out of vital routes to safety and security". Logic follows that, "without routes to safe accommodation, victims face a stark choice: either be trapped in abuse or face homelessness and destitution."[19] This blunt "choice" can lead, as it did with Aaden, to perpetrators exploiting NRPF to further threaten and control their partner without settlement rights in the UK. Sometimes victims' limited English language skills and lack of knowledge of the national system and legal rights mean that perpetrators are further emboldened to weaponize immigration status with impunity.

Feminist geographer Rosa dos Ventos Lopes Heimer argues that migrant women in such circumstances are victims of "state-sponsored interpersonal violence which flows from immigration policies and which exposes certain gendered and racialised bodies to harm". In other words, the distinction between state violence and domestic abuse becomes fuzzy: "abusive men reassert their border authority by projecting national sovereign power" over women. NRPF can be viewed in this guise as "a major internal bordering technology of legal abandonment" that takes effect in "statutory destitution", namely the denial of life-saving welfare support and public services.[20] As gender equality expert Halliki Voolma puts it simply, "the aim of immigration control precedes that of ending violence against women".[21]

It is also possible that Casho was wrongly advised that she would be denied access to public funds if she left Aaden. Although not without limitations, those on spousal visas suffering domestic abuse can access support via the Migrant Victims of Domestic Abuse Concession (formerly the Destitution Domestic Violence Concession or DDVC). The Angelou Centre, which provides services for black and minoritized women across the northeast of England, has shown however that 70 per cent of referrals into their refuges and violence against women and girls (VAWG) services in 2020–21 involved women categorized as having NRPF but who should have been eligible to access public funds via what was then the DDVC.[22] This highlights how domestic abuse is further compounded by deficient levels of legal knowledge among some of the very institutions that are supposed to protect victims.

Schools, often under their own financial and staffing pressures, have become the front line of the housing crisis and are crucial in supporting families. In the state school sector, 49 per cent of teachers work at a school with children who are homeless or who have become homeless in the last year.[23] The headteacher of the school Casho's children attended was one of the only people she knew and trusted. Casho was supported by her to make an Indefinite Leave to Remain application. Before being granted, however, the Covid-19 pandemic hit and, like Irhaa, Casho was trapped in the flat with her husband. "It was not good." The violence intensified, her insomnia worsened, and her stress spiralled: "I wanna take it out. Everything out of my mind." Casho recalls telling a (male) GP that she felt suicidal. He responded, "Don't say this, what would happen to your kids? And if social services hear you talking like this, they will think you are stressed out and maybe you can't have your kids. Go home, everything will be fine." Casho left the appointment in floods of tears. "The GP said they couldn't help me, and basically told me to pick myself up", Christine also painfully recalled a similar encounter. Academic research has evidenced how a lack of understanding from GPs about the seriousness of domestic abuse is putting women and children at a serious risk of harm.[24] In addition to having more compassion and understanding of the predicaments and risks faced living with violence, Casho's and Christine's life experiences underscore the importance of the need for GP training to better identify and signpost patients experiencing domestic abuse to wider support.[25]

On the day Casho's Indefinite Leave to Remain status was granted in 2022, Aaden found out and reacted violently. He began beating Casho across her head. "He said 'I will kill you. I will take the kids. You are gonna die today'." During the attack Casho managed to call the school and leave the phone line on so they could hear what was happening. The police arrived and arrested Aaden. Casho and her children were moved into temporary accommodation. "When the police came I was told I couldn't stay in the flat . . . 'it's not in your name' they said." It transpired that Aaden had lied to her. The council tenancy was not under their joint names, only his. "*Everything* was in his name", she emphasized. In Christine's life expert testimony in parliament, and then in our interview with her subsequently, she elaborated on how she had been deceived too:

> I kept on asking HIM to go, and he was having none of it. And I was unaware at the time that my name wasn't even on the [council] tenancy. We'd waited five years to be housed, so we had already been in a form of temporary accommodation for a couple of years, bidding, and then we got housed. I couldn't see it at the time, as we settled in, I thought right I can go back to work now, my daughter is starting reception class . . . it was about after a year when I got a job that he became a lot more controlling.

For Christine, her partner's restriction and sabotage through money constrained her options to leave. But leave she did, with essential logistical support from Women's Aid:

> I had got to that stage where if I don't leave he is going to kill me, them, or all three of us. And so literally, I had to do it, you never think you are that person, and I said it in my story [in parliament], I didn't think I

> was that person, that I was a victim of domestic violence. But over the years when you reflect back you think ohhh ... oh yeah, actually this is my story.

While Christine and Casho were freed from their abusive husbands, both entered another sort of punitive relationship, this time with debt. An Argos credit card was pasted by Casho onto her collage. It smothered the damp high-rise block she once called home.

Disbelieved

> You turn on survival mode. How can I explain it? You aren't living, you're just breathing... I woke up in the morning because I had no choice. If I didn't have my kids, I wouldn't be here today. A million per cent.

A dog barked as we were invited into Jade's house. We walked through the narrow hall where the staircase has become home to an ominous stack of bills about to topple over. Moving to the lounge, we squished onto the sofa to talk. Jade, then a mum of two in her early thirties, explained that her dog Hector had become a big part of her recovery from three years of life in temporary accommodation. Developing anxiety, depression and agoraphobia during this time, the dog got her out of the house each day and offered companionship and love. The Covid-19 pandemic had worsened her "hiding away for so long", which again made Hector a welcomed source of emotional support.

Living in permanent social housing for a year with Hector, her suicidal thoughts had abated. These suicidal thoughts, including one suicide attempt, she believes was the result of "the system that pushed me to do it". Scholars Ruth Aitken and Vanessa Munro explain that "[t]hose trapped by domestic violence can feel so hopeless that they believe the only way out is suicide". Suicide is more likely when "feelings of defeat and entrapment exist alongside beliefs that neither rescue nor escape are possible".[26] Ninety-eight people who have committed suicide in the 12 months to March 2024 are believed to have done so because of domestic abuse.[27]

The debt trap that Jade was still trying to find her way out of was not just laid by the perpetrator. It is, as Jade points out (and Casho found out), maintained and governed by a wider bureaucratic system, or Byzantine labyrinth, that women must navigate to seek safety from. For Jade, although supposedly past the traumatic years of domestic abuse and life in temporary accommodation, "survival mode" was proving hard to move on from. Her self-confessed adrenaline-filled journey was now spiked with incalculable debts waiting for her on the staircase to open and male bailiffs aggressively rapping their fists against her front door demanding repayment.

Jade fretted at the unquantifiable figure she still owed given the high interest rates much of her borrowing was pegged to. Catalogue debt had been run up to pay for her children's birthdays and Christmases, festivities that she felt loathed and guilty as a mother to deny them. "I couldn't even afford to feed my children", Jade noted, let alone buy them gifts to celebrate. Weighing heavily on many of the women we spoke with was a gendered sense of responsibility and motherly guilt expressed to compensate for their children's lack of a permanent home. This involved making birthdays and Christmases as special as possible and, as it did for Jade, translated into spending on gifts through store cards or "buy now, pay later" credit suppliers such as Klarna.

Loan shark lenders were also an expensive crutch Jade turned to, particularly when living in temporary accommodation. They are essentially unregulated illegal lenders who in Jade's case charged her 50 per cent interest on a £700 loan. Jade said she was pressured to repay the loan, cash in hand, each week. It was "scary" given they knew where she lived and regularly used threats to ensure repayment. "I will never do that to myself again", she told us. The loan shark threats retraumatized her by mirroring the intimidation she had faced in her previous relationship. Although the loan shark debts are now settled, she believes she still owes money to 40–45 companies and people. There is certainly at least £900 of council tax arrears to deal with. Debt had just piled on in her attempts to sustain family life, and her mental health is rapidly declining again.

From the age of seven Jade, of mixed ethnicity, grew up with her nan. Later, she worked as a carer of disabled children and moved between 2006 and 2015 to a series of four private rented houses. All were "falling to pieces". In one property, sewage was leaking, contaminating one of the gardens. For six years, Jade was in a relationship with Mark, the father of their two children. Jade's story is one (like Casho) of becoming homeless and debt trapped because of domestic abuse and the state failing to act. "He took all of my money. You see it happened slowly over a period of time. He didn't put his hands on me for a long time. It was verbal. Then he'd throw stuff at me. A tin of beans in my face. But he didn't put his hands on me." Here Jade is evoking the idea that domestic abuse is, as feminist geographers have explored, a form of "slow violence" that is incremental, continual and often rendered publicly invisible.[28] Jade went on to describe the tactics her partner used to control her further, strategically instilling a sense of fault and shame when she questioned his actions: "Apparently, it was *me* overreacting, *I'm* being dramatic. So then you think, *am I*?" Again, Jade and women in similar situations are made to feel guilty, to feel responsible, for the violence suffered, and for debt accrued through and in its aftermath. Christine reflected on this with us: "when someone betrays me [like her violent partner did] I get heartfelt disappointment, and I think 'what did I do', not blaming them, 'what did I do, what could I have done better?' ". The internalization and personalization of blame is part and parcel of the torment that can be felt by victims of domestic abuse and those in problem debt.

Self-blame and the isolation that these experiences create are distressing. No one knew what Jade was suffering, and even when the couple had company in the house the violence didn't stop. "Sometimes it was just a look when his friends were around. The look of 'get the fuck upstairs', he'd be kicking me up the stairs while his friends were back downstairs." Calling the police got her nowhere.

> Unless something's happening there and then, it doesn't really matter. This is why I didn't go to the police. Because unless I rung when it was actually happening, there and then, it's just dismissed. So unless I said, he's got his hands around my throat, they wouldn't come. I remember ringing once when he was kicking my door in, and they said somebody would be with me. Like obviously it's classed as an emergency, and he'd already beat me up. He'd left and come back. And they said somebody had come, and I got a phone call about four days later ... sorry, nobody had come. And I thought, you know what, I had my

> daughter screaming and shaking in the corner of the room, and I was panicking, thinking he's going to get back in after he just beat me up in front of her. And they didn't even turn up. So, from that time, I never rang them again.

The double speak was not lost on Jade, that publicly at least the police took domestic abuse seriously, but in practice they were often absent: "It's like, lets put posters around, put a smile on our faces. But when you need us, we're not there." In Greater Manchester, service deterioration was uncovered in an inspection by His Majesty's Inspectorate of Constabulary and Fire and Rescue Services:

> A matter of especially serious concern is the failure to record a high proportion of violent crime, including domestic abuse and behavioural crimes such as harassment, stalking and coercive controlling behaviour. And in many cases the force does not investigate these unrecorded offences or provide safeguarding to victims. This is potentially leaving many victims at risk. It is important that these shortcomings are put right as a matter of urgency.[29]

Jade's poor experiences of the police locally – as acknowledged in this inspection – are more nationally felt. Based on research with over 1,000 victims of domestic abuse, Victim Support painted a grim picture of police inaction in the UK. Nearly a quarter of respondents reported an instance of domestic abuse to the police three times or more before appropriate action was taken; more than one in ten respondents said that they did not feel appropriate action was ever taken; and when reporting an instance of domestic abuse, almost half of Black and ethnic minority respondents felt that the police treated them differently to other people because of their ethnic background or heritage.[30] Accusations of racism and misogyny in the police force in different parts of the country are also linked to a decline in public trust, especially among women and minority groups.[31]

In 2017 Jade packed as many belongings as she could in the middle of the night and fled with her children. A friend had noticed Mark's behaviour and urged her to leave. "He was very secretive [not] doing things in front of people and I still to this day think that if he hadn't accidentally been seen by my friend, I would still be with him now." "I had no idea where I was gonna go." Jade spent the first year after she fled sofa-surfing with her children. "Sometimes I had to sleep upright so my kids could lie down", and her belongings and the kids' school uniforms were strewn "here, there, and everywhere". She then sought housing assistance from the council. But this was traumatizing in itself:

> You're in the worst position in your life, like some people have been through awful things to get where they got to, and to walk in, sat there thinking I'm going to be sent away. I've got nowhere to go with my two kids. I had a baby and a little boy. I went through domestic violence. When I got seen they [the council staff] said to me because I've not notified it to anybody, just been living with it, I've not told the police or anything like that, I can't be telling the truth.

Jade's experiences of domestic abuse had been dismissed and she was branded a liar for not seeking prior help from the police (see Alison's testimony at the start of Chapter 4 for further evidence of this happening). Particularly for women like Casho who are categorized as having NRPF, Women's Aid have found additionally that women are being refused support, told that the domestic abuse they have been experiencing is "not serious enough" and informed that they do not have "priority need for housing".[32] Disbelief and the denial of assistance are part of what makes the debt trap a patriarchal construct that keeps women living in homes where violence goes unchallenged, financial autonomy is undercut and men's power and agency is ascendant. It has to stop.

Stalked

As with Jade, even when women have managed to leave violent partners, the family homelessness that often follows continues to feed the debt trap. Some women are stalked not only by ongoing debt that follows them around, as with Jade and her growing pile of bills, but by ex-partners trying to find them, which then can lead to further debt as they are forced to flee, again and again. Many victims describe debt as a form of repunishment that stays with them long after the domestic abuse ends. Afterlives of domestic abuse aren't always possible while outstanding debt remains unpaid and debt mounts up.

Women's hyper-mobility is also costly financially and emotionally. Zofia, a Polish-born White woman in her early forties, has carried these costs of displacement, churn and fear for years. She has been trapped in movement, a forced migration of sorts. According to geographer Janet Bowstead, domestic abuse victims can be thought of as internally displaced persons in the United Kingdom.[33] This way of seeing goes against the prevailing orthodoxy: that displaced people impacted by human rights infringements are located "elsewhere", in the Global South. Yet tens of thousands of women like Zofia are undertaking hidden journeys across England and the UK more widely.

Bartek, Zofia's ex-partner and father to her two sons, had a long history of emotional and economic violence: "he was very jealous from the start of our relationship. He said, you don't need to work ... I was too young to understand that it was a trap. So he could fully control me." In dismissing Zofia's keenness to seek employment, she identifies how her partner worked to weaken the possibility of her financial autonomy, thus binding her to him. Bartek had set the trap. When her eldest son turned four, Bartek began to hit Zofia. Turning to the police led to her moving into a refuge in the south of England. Like Christine, she left for the refuge with only one bag. She has since "run everywhere from him", resulting in two stays in refuges and multiple other stays in temporary accommodation.

As she points out, "the whole system is wrong". In the feedback and discussion group we ran at the baby bank towards the end of the study, Zofia and several of the women (including Jade) took "the system" to task for placing the expectation and responsibility on women rather than their abusers to flee. In conversation with Zofia, another participant, Laura, reflected: "You're the one who has to go through domestic abuse and social services meetings. And it's the abuser that is walking free. Coming and going as *he* pleases! You're there suffering ... it's absolutely shocking!" Zofia vigorously agreed. "They should come for that guy. Not me! I'm the one running! And what does it do to the kids?" With bitter irony in her voice, she explained, "and then you get to a refuge, you are told, you are the winner, because you are a survivor! *Excuse me*?!" "When every time in the refuge, it's the same story, there is something wrong." While there is no ultimate consensus, the label of "victim" is commonly eschewed given its connotation with helplessness and passivity. "Survivor", in contrast, is viewed by many feminist scholars and activists as minimizing these connotations and instead emphasizing resilience and even empowerment. However, as Zofia scoffs, there is a risk too that being called a "survivor" does not meaningfully convey her torturous experiences. The cascading impacts of domestic abuse and system failures flowed like a torrent through her still unfolding story. "You have *everything* on *you*", she emphasized.

Only a few days before our last meeting with Zofia in October 2023, Bartek began harassing her about custody access to her children after "two years of quiet". "It's my right", he demanded. This is not unusual. Attempts to continue violence and control are often pursued through child contact. According to Zofia, despite four court orders against him in the past, she has again spoken to the police with the hope of action being taken. But the court orders had expired, the police responded – "like, come on!" – Zofia exclaimed in frustration. Her exasperation stemmed from past encounters with the state. The first time she contacted the police, when she left Bartek and he continued to harass her, she was reassured she would be safe and protected. "But then the officer said, I spoke with Bartek and he's a nice guy, he just wants to see his kids." A woman in social services came to the same conclusion. "Every time it's the same, it is the same . . . social services should have more knowledge about domestic abuse."

Over and over, women's experiences of domestic abuse and the debt trap they have been pulled into are delegitimized. Here Zofia is raising the minimization and denial of her experiences at the hands of a manipulative perpetrator and the naive cum complicit local authority and police force:

> On the police website it says domestic violence is very important. It's not only physical, it's emotional blah blah blah. It's a crime. But for me, after what I have been through . . . he's still free despite the harassment. I'm in another domestic violence situation with the system. You ask for help, they say we cannot help you, here's a number, you make 50 phone calls, call, call, call, and nothing.

"The system" is trapping women in cycles, twists and turns, of hope and despair, assistance and abandonment, that undermines their ability to seek an afterlife from violence. When Zofia moved into the first refuge hundreds of miles from home, her Universal Credit was stopped "because I changed places". She was told to make a new claim, "so for six weeks I didn't have any money, all we had was food from the refuge and the food bank". The detrimental impacts of an official (but often exceeded) five-week delay between making a claim and being in receipt of benefits worsened Zofia's financial situation and she struggled in the refuge without money to make adjustments for her son's celiac disease. Given the lack of any financial reserves to draw on, lengthy waits for a first Universal Credit payment are leaving claimants deeper in debt as they try to cope with the delay. Philip Alston, a past UN special rapporteur on extreme poverty and human rights, found in his official visit to the United Kingdom that situations like Zofia's were both widespread and damaging. He reported that "this 'waiting period,' which actually often takes up to 12 weeks, pushes many who may already be in crisis into debt, rent arrears, and serious hardship, requiring them to sacrifice food or heat".[34] A debt trap is born from the punitiveness and carelessness of the temporal in welfare design.

After three months in the refuge, Zofia was given permanent social housing in what she lovingly called a "beautiful village". But this peace would be short-lived: "I had been there only six months, and my ex-partner found out the address. I was so scared, he threatened to throw acid on my face, that he knew people everywhere who could do it." Zofia was forced to move again within 48 hours, to a refuge in another part of England. "I had totally lost myself, who I am", by this point. Out of fear she changed her hair colour, "I was so afraid he found me ... I didn't feel safe in the house". Zofia was advised by a women's support charity to switch off the location services on her mobile phone, after they suspected that Bartek had been tracking her through this form of "tech abuse". "I still don't know how he found me; he knew exactly where I lived." The spatial and temporal hold of perpetrators is tightened through technology-enabled coercive control: "digital technologies enable abusers to more efficiently and effectively coercively control survivors *anywhere* and *at any time,* including after the relationship has ended".[35] In England, the perpetration of domestic abuse via the use of technology, especially smartphones, has become more common. However, research has established not only that many statutory and volunteer services are not equipped to respond but also that domestic abuse legislation does not reflect evolving risks.[36]

At her son's behest, Zofia eventually moved from the refuge back to the north of England and began living in temporary accommodation, initially a hotel. Her story is one of being stalked by her ex-partner and increasingly by debt. Leaving for the second refuge at such short notice meant she couldn't give proper notice on her tenancy (she went on to owe £3,000 in rent arrears as a consequence) and she is still being chased for missed council tax payments. Zofia also continued to pay for the gas, electricity and internet in her old house long after she fled. Debt had taken a life of its own. "There's no compassion", she challenged. Debt still haunts Zofia and, like Christine, she now has an IVA in place given the range of creditors she owes. An IVA allows borrowers to restructure their debts and repay them in a way they can afford. It can have a negative effect on a person's credit score, which can make it more difficult in the future to secure a credit loan.

As part of the IVA, or similar Debt Relief Order (DRO), it is usual for the name and address of the debtor to be made public on the Individual Insolvency Register, a practice that puts domestic abuse victims at risk. BBC News, for example, ran an article on a domestic abuse victim in Wales who was £10,000 in debt, some taken out by her ex-partner in her name. Upon leaving her partner, "Helen" sought a DRO. Despite fleeing to a refuge and move five times to evade him, Helen's name and address were published on the insolvency register.[37] It is little known that in order to stop an address showing, victims need to apply for a Person at Risk of Violence order from the courts. The onus is again placed on the abused to protect themselves and to ask for permission to even do so.

In Zofia's case, her story of domestic abuse, debt and family homelessness unfurls still further. Because of her rent arrears Zofia could not bid for a permanent social housing tenancy while in temporary accommodation. She was stuck, having been told "there is no chance" of bidding because of this debt. Advocating for herself to the council she previously had the tenancy with in the south of England, the rent arrears were eventually reduced to less than £1,000, which enabled her to start bidding. Chapter 4 delves deeper into this element of the debt trap, in which domestic abuse victims are being cruelly caught as a consequence of local authority rules on housing allocation.

Forced back

We hugged Irhaa after passing through security at Portcullis House, the home of MPs' offices and meeting rooms in Westminster. Irhaa had travelled for the day to London in October 2023 to tell her story to the All-Party Parliamentary Group (APPG) for Households in Temporary Accommodation. At the APPG we were launching our research report.[38] Together with Irhaa, we waited upstairs outside our allotted room. All perched on the regulation green banquette seating, we gave Irhaa a physical copy of *The Debt Trap* report we had just finished writing. Under the painted portraits and watchful eyes of William Hague, Charles Kennedy and Tony Blair, Irhaa intently read her summated life story. She smiled, she was happy with her pseudonym, a name she'd always loved. Tears gently made their way down her cheeks: ones of pride and recognition, she told us. The shedding of a few tears before we entered the room made her feel ready. Some of the emotion of the day had apparently been washed away.

The APPG meeting was held in person and online. Given the risks of identification, Irhaa was carefully positioned to the side of the computer screen so she couldn't be seen by the virtual attendees. Around a large rectangular wooden table, we sat next to Irhaa and directly opposite from the then parliamentary under secretary of state for the Department for Levelling Up, Housing and Communities, MP Felicity Buchan. The Labour MPs Rebecca Long-Bailey of Salford and co-sponsor of the APPG, Siobhain McDonagh of Mitcham and Morden, were to our right. After presenting the key findings of the research, Christine gave her life expert testimony before Irhaa turned to hers.

Irhaa's freedom from Auraq had been short-lived. More than a year on from our second interview together in summer 2022, she had had no choice but to go back. "I couldn't get back on my feet – making the sums add up is impossible." The Universal Credit she received was insufficient given the rising cost of living, made worse by the two-child benefit cap, a detriment which is more likely to affect Black, Asian and ethnic minority families.[39]

Long-running financial anxieties and outstanding debts had resulted in diagnosed depression, Irhaa told the room:

> After three years of being on this journey, my mental health was affected, and I had no choice but to move back in with my husband because of the financial situation. He pays for me to live in a separate place with my children, however, I have to be careful. I must keep playing happy families with someone I hate; someone I am petrified of just so he can financially support me and my children. He has all the power, and he can decide one week to just not pay for the rent or food.

The debt trap had proved too strong, too hard to escape. The precarious economics of everyday life wedded her once more to her abusive husband. An "afterlife" from her abuser was not possible for now. Prior to the APPG meeting, we had met Irhaa privately to understand what had happened in the intervening time since we had last spoken. Resonating with her APPG testimony several weeks later, she reflected, "I'm kind of reliving my past with my abuser. But it's not like I have a choice." Looking almost nauseous, she said: "even now, sometimes when he comes closer to me, I have to fake the love if that makes sense, even though I am full of resentment. If I don't, he goes funny and stroppy and doesn't want to pay for things. I'm having to do what I have to do." To reiterate, the debt trap cannot be understood only through its damning financial calculus but through the visceral body and intimate relations that it puts pressures on.

A primary reason why women, including Irhaa, return to an abusive partner are the financial barriers to leading independent lives. England is a debt trap nation that has structurally caught Irhaa's lifeworld and so many other women in its unrelenting web. The lack of choice that Irhaa directly references speaks to her entrapment by her perpetrator and a failing state. A client of the London-based charity Furnishing Futures expresses this in the frankest of terms in an Instagram post: "Poverty is killing women like me, because we can't afford to leave."[40] An average of 1.2 women *per week* are killed by a male partner or ex-partner in the United Kingdom.[41] The debt trap is dangerous and at times fatal.

Irhaa survived, but she is now being punished again. Her experiences, like those of other women we met, speak to tensions between "having temporary *safety from* violence and *freedom to* live as they choose".[42] Debt chips away at women's autonomy to make decisions in their own interests, visions and desires. While women may find safety by leaving an abusive relationship, this does not necessarily mean that they are free from financial difficulties. As this chapter has shown, debt stalks, it haunts, and it forces decisions that may seem unfathomable to those who do not understand, or are not compassionate to, its burden.

Safeguarding and VAWG minister in the Labour government, MP Jess Phillips has said she believes the long-standing lack of prioritization of domestic abuse against women and girls makes it the "Cinderella" of crimes; in other words, it is left festering at home and overlooked.[43] Many of the women we met in our research had personal experience of this neglect. In the run-up to the July 2024 election, the Labour leader (and now prime minister), Keir Starmer, said he wanted to "imagine a society where violence against women is stamped out everywhere" and set the ambition of halving VAWG in a decade. In many organizations' eyes, however, the government's 2024 Autumn Budget did not include enough detail about what funding had been committed to this task.[44] Stable and sufficient funding for life-saving services such as refuges is mission-critical, but this needs to be accompanied by more fundamental shifts. What Irhaa's life experiences tell us is that debt can bind women once more to their abuser, undermining not only freedom but safety. In a failing state, choice to live free from interpersonal and financial domination is not viable and open to all. Not only this, but as Alison's testimony (which follows this chapter) confirms, the housing crisis and lack of affordable housing supply is a threat to women's ability to leave a violent relationship. To dismantle the debt trap means overturning sexism, misogyny and deep-rooted intersectional inequalities and power imbalances between women and men in England today.

ALISON

Former President of the Chartered Institute of Housing (CIH)
16 Days of Activism Against Domestic Abuse
The Social Housing Roundtable
26 November 2024 [online][45]

We find it very difficult institutionally [as housing professionals] to step back, and say, well actually, is there something more complex behind this [homelessness]. We have reporting systems that say tick box A or tick box B. It is the same with rent arrears, so as soon as someone is in significant rent arrears, they are on a little pathway that ends with one of those letters with red writing on (that people put in the bin), that actually says, you know, you are going to go to court.

You [as a housing professional] are already on a way of thinking, whereas we know from the report that the CIH Cymru did ten years ago, that said domestic abuse, is one of the leading drivers of rent arrears. So, it is standing back and using professional judgement, looking at relationships and households in the round, and STOP expecting victims to be as pure as the driven snow, because if I was experiencing things that people are experiencing on a day-to-day basis, I do not think it would bring the best out in me. So why do we assume that of everybody else? . . .

I think that one of the things that dawned on me gradually, was, not just the fact that housing is where most domestic abuse takes place, and it can be a solution [for a domestic abuse survivor to move], but also how it can be a cause. And I think the housing shortage has contributed to living arrangements . . . meeting someone and moving in with them three months later, you will both save something on the rent as you only have one rent to pay . . . and then suddenly it all goes a bit wrong, the relationship needs to finish at that point, but housing keeps you together . . . there aren't enough places for people to live.

I cannot imagine the stress of working in a London local authority homelessness department when you have no accommodation. When temporary accommodation is full, and your local authority is going broke. So, we begin to see rationing take place, because that is just what happens.

I am beginning to see over the last three years, more anecdotes of housing professionals saying, and this is dreadful, obviously, "oh I think people reporting domestic abuse are only saying it in order to get housing". And it is one of those issues we need to face head-on. And I don't think we've had that conversation in the housing sector yet. No one goes into housing to make that kind of stigmatized judgement, and it is a symptom of an absolutely broken system. But, the fact that people in housing are saying that women in housing are going . . . it is humiliating to report abuse to a faceless bureaucrat, it is not something anyone does for a bit of a laugh, OK, it can be traumatizing, you are asked to replay your trauma, time after time, reporting the same thing to different people, and then if our judgement is, "you are only saying that to get a transfer, prove it", we are going back 30–40 years to the late 1970s, 1980s, when you literally had to have a black eye.

We've seen local authorities ask for a letter, it is so Kafkaesque, a letter from the perpetrator where he will agree to what he can do. I mean, it is heartbreaking, and it is unprofessional, and this is where we need training, and sort of, the backbone from the organization, [saying] these are our values, and this is what we stand for, and this is not how we are going to do business.

*

YOU CAN'T BID BECAUSE YOU'RE IN THE RED

PAST DUE

FINAL NOTICE

PAST DUE

PAY NOW

4

Imprisoned by debt in temporary accommodation

Arriving at Orla's temporary accommodation and waiting for her to answer the door, we noticed a letterbox mounted on the wall, stuffed with what looked like bills peeking out, as if trying to make themselves known. After a short while, a tired-looking woman in her mid-twenties opened the door. Orla offered to give us the "grand tour", as she called it, but seeing as there were just three rooms, this didn't take long. A kitchen barely big enough to stand, let alone cook in, a tiny windowless bathroom and a room that acts as a combined living and bedroom where Orla and her baby daughter have been living for over a year. As Orla's daughter is under one year old, she does not technically "count" as a person according to the council's housing policy, meaning she is not accounted for in overcrowding policy or statistics. Orla has done her best to make the living-bedroom functional and pleasant for her and her daughter – in the corner, a travel cot doubles up as a colourful ball pit, and every day Orla blows up an air bed to sleep on, "I put it down, and then tonight I'm going to blow it back up again!" Every inch of the room is made use of, with IKEA storage units she bought tucked behind the door to try and create more room for her daughter to play. But no amount of organization can hide the limited space and poor quality of the accommodation.

Before Orla's daughter was born, she had been living in a rundown private rented property, piecing together her rent through a range of zero-hour contract jobs.

> The rent was only £400 [per month], but the house was rundown when I moved into it. It's like a cat had lived in there feral for weeks with nobody looking after it . . . I spent about four grand . . . putting all the flooring down, painting it, doing everything, made it my home. But the landlord would not lift a finger to do absolutely anything in the house.

Having been raised in the care system, Orla was used to looking after herself. But work started drying up. Less casual work was being given out by the burger chain she relied on for income. It got harder to find enough hours to meet her rent payments, and she started falling behind. Orla's landlord moved to issue an eviction notice the day before she received her first payment from the Job Centre. Now pregnant and with nowhere else to move to, she refused to leave, running up £2,400 of rent arrears as a consequence. Finally evicted, Orla had needed to escape the property anyway after her ex-partner had recently attacked her there. While this was far from the first time this had happened, she was pregnant now: the stakes were higher.

Fearing for the safety of her unborn baby, Orla hoped that moving would protect them from her violent ex-partner. After the eviction, she sofa-surfed at friends' places for a few months, knowing that this couldn't go on for much longer, especially as time went on and her due date loomed near. Orla went to the council, who placed her in a hotel: "there was rats in there. It was full of junkies. I was heavily pregnant. I was on the top floor as well, with four flights of stairs to get to my room." Orla was then moved to her current temporary accommodation. She describes the small flat as a "prison" she is stuck in.

Rent arrears pushed Orla into homelessness, and now it is keeping her trapped there. Until she pays back a significant amount of her debts, she's not eligible to even begin the process of bidding for permanent social housing. She explained: "they've [the council] said you can't bid because you're in the red". Thousands of mothers across England are being caught in a Kafkaesque nightmare in which, at every step, they are punished for being in debt. Debt not only causes family homelessness but also keeps families trapped in temporary accommodation through inhumane housing allocation rules that need proper scrutiny. This is yet another example of where families have not fallen into this debt trap; they have been actively pulled into it.

As we recounted earlier, the word "prison" was used by many of the women we spoke with to characterize their stays in temporary accommodation. Stays in emergency accommodation should not legally exceed six weeks, but between September and July 2024, 3,470 families in England surpassed this statutory limit in bed and breakfast (B&B) hotels.[1] This translates to 64 per cent of all children (5,400) in this unsuitable accommodation being trapped beyond the six-week limit. In our previous writing we called the increased state use of and reliance of states on hotels for housing the "hotelisation of the housing crisis".[2] Hotels are becoming what urban studies scholars refer to as "institutions of containment".[3]

This chapter brings to light the inner lives of homeless families in England who are imprisoned by debt in temporary accommodation. For mothers and their children, housing-related debt is a triple jeopardy, often arising in situations of domestic abuse, causing family homelessness and then trapping them in temporary accommodation. Evidencing these connections, we elaborate on the argument made in previous chapters, that temporary accommodation can be thought of as the debtors' prison of the twenty-first century. In this chapter we introduce Orla, Jessica, Belle, Laura and Taniyah, and return to Jade's and Zofia's journeys. Through their stories, we bring to the fore families' traumatic experiences of interfacing with housing bureaucracy, and how blame for indebtedness is lain at the (temporary, poor quality) door of mothers.

Abandoned

Often in combination with domestic abuse, having rent arrears in the private rented sector was one of the main causes of indebtedness among the women we met. The latest quarterly figures for England reveal that 40 per cent of all households who were owed what is called a homelessness prevention duty[4] from their local authority between July and September 2024 was because of rent arrears.[5] This trend is unsurprising given the extortionate and still rising cost of private renting in the UK. For the same quarterly period, the property website Rightmove listed record-breaking average rents of £1,344 per calendar month outside of London, and an eye-watering £2,631 per calendar month in the capital.[6] By comparison, people on Universal Credit are seeing a fall in their already paltry income. According to analysis by the New Economics Foundation, despite Universal Credit rising in line with inflation in 2024, people are likely to be £670 worse off than in the preceding year. This is in part because cost-of-living payments, introduced in 2022 to offset spiralling household costs, ended in February 2024.[7] The Local Housing Allowance (LHA), the rate used to calculate the maximum amount of housing support for Universal Credit claimants, has also not kept up with the record-breaking costs of renting. There are estimated to be 440,000 households with children whose housing support no longer covers the costs of their rent.[8] In London, just 5 per cent of private rented sector properties have rents low enough to be covered by the LHA rate.[9] For households caught by this gap, these figures seed fertile ground for debt accrual.

Despite this, the Labour government's first Autumn Budget saw Chancellor Rachel Reeves announcing that the LHA rate would be frozen from 2025. This freeze follows a decade of rising rental costs and the LHA failing to keep step, and according to the Institute for Public Policy Research, this will push 90,000 more families into financial hardship by 2026.[10] Low-income renters are yet again left to struggle with the differential between the housing support they are given and the private rents they are struggling to pay. The blueprint for a failing state risks being reproduced, namely families being pulled into the debt trap through circumstances out of their control. Writing in *Prospect* magazine, the writer Tom Clark laments:

> It may be galling – and even dismissed as a sticking plaster – to increase payments which line the pockets of private landlords, while merely stopping things from getting worse for people in need. And yet until we can break out of the housing system we're currently stuck with, this is the only way to get a grip on that ruinous bill for emergency shelter.[11]

Government itself needs to take greater control of the wheel in order to break out of this system. There needs to be a fundamental rethink on how to deal with and regulate a profit-driven runaway private rented sector that has, in effect, been subsidized by the state through its benefits system for decades now. As Nick Bano points out, Thatcher's government shifted local authorities from direct providers of housing to the providers of housing benefit (as it was called at the time) to be used in the private rented sector, with the effect that landlords took the driving seat. They raised rents, with benefit levels having to rise as a result. "This should have been obvious from the start", Bano chastises as he charts the vast transfer of state wealth to private landlords and the raising of rents that left the state in a position of "underwriting a large part of the national rent bill".[12]

As we explored in Chapter 3, financial strains on families who rent can be especially acute in situations of domestic abuse when mothers' access to money is controlled by their partner. Jessica is a Black woman in her early thirties, mother to her ten-year-old son Archie. Living in a private rented property in Greater Manchester with Archie and her partner, what limited money she had was usually taken out of her hands. As with most of our research participants, Jessica was economically, as well as physically, abused by her now ex-partner. He demanded the majority of the monthly Universal Credit payment – all that she managed to keep for herself was £20 per week in child benefit as it was paid separately into her account. Jessica tried her best to store what little she did have away, paying it into a Credit Union so she could access it whenever she might need to. However, she had to keep dipping into it to cover essentials, meaning that her secret stash soon disappeared. On top of this, her partner wasn't contributing to the rent or bills, and she soon fell into rent, council tax and utility arrears. Desperately trying to keep afloat, Jessica asked for loans from friends and family, but it wasn't enough. Her landlady told her that the arrears had become too big and evicted them from the property. By the time of her eviction, Jessica estimated that she had around £1,000 of debts, none of which her ex-partner took any responsibility for. Mothers like Jessica are being abandoned, "left holding the baby" and dealing with record-breaking rent increases by abusive ex-partners and a state that remains fixated on economic orthodoxy that privileges the wants of landlords over social needs.

When we met Jessica, we learned too that she had limited opportunity for any financial autonomy through paid employment. She had been the primary carer for her ill grandmother for most of her adult life and prior to this, since primary school, had been in the care of the local authority. Jessica and Orla, who both spent their childhoods largely in care, face a "double whammy" when it comes to housing costs and risks of homelessness. Become, a charity for children in care and young care leavers, found that 9 per cent of care leavers aged 18–25 in 2023 were statutorily assessed as being homeless or facing homelessness. This compares to an estimated 0.97 per cent of non-care-experienced young people who were either homeless or at risk of homelessness in the same period.[13] For the 100,000 children in care by 2025, multiple educational and other systemic disadvantages are curtailing future life successes. Jessica, for example, contends with compounding intersectional disadvantages; data from England and Wales show that Black African and Caribbean children, particularly with a single parent, are overrepresented in the social care population and Black adults who were once in care are the least likely of any ethnicity to be homeowners.[14]

Refused

Given ballooning rental costs and LHA rates that are failing to keep pace, many families in England have little choice but to live in poor quality, even uninhabitable, housing. In 2025 the Renters' Rights Bill (a reincarnation of the previous Conservative government's Renters' Reform Bill) is expected to become law. It will introduce a Decent Homes Standard to the private rented sector and is envisaged to give local authorities the power and resources to enforce these standards. It is badly needed. The English Housing Survey shows that 990,000 occupied private rented sector dwellings (23 per cent) are estimated to fail the Decent Homes Standard, proportionally more than any other tenure.[15] To make matters worse, it is believed that 14 per cent of private rented sector homes are unsafe. Households in receipt of housing benefits are more likely to be living in private rental accommodation with a dangerous hazard than those who do not receive benefits.[16]

The Renters' Rights Bill will abolish Section 21 evictions, which allow landlords to evict tenants without any reason needed. This is essential given that private tenants have extremely limited legal rights, even when the home they rent is in a barely liveable condition. It is widely documented that tenants run the risk of being evicted if they complain about issues, including major health risks such as damp, mould and vermin. Research conducted by Citizens Advice revealed that private tenants who formally complain about issues with their property such as mould and damp were twice as likely to receive a no-fault eviction (Section 21) notice from their landlord.[17]

This was the case for Belle, a White British woman in her mid-thirties. She was living in a privately rented two-bedroom house with her three children. It seemed relatively affordable at first: most of the rent was covered by her housing benefit, with Belle making up the difference through work. Although she was initially pleased as the house was in a nice suburb of Greater Manchester, the – quite literal – cracks soon began to appear. There were huge fissures growing along the walls and ceiling, gaps opening in the floors and along the skirting boards, mould and damp, and tiles falling off the ceiling: "I was paranoid, like is this ceiling going to fall in? . . . There was 90 cracks in the house by the time I left." Alongside the clear structural issues, Belle soon discovered that there was a mouse infestation too. She contacted her landlord, who visited but dismissed all of her concerns, telling her there was nothing wrong with the house: "obviously I'm not daft . . . [but] they just dismiss you and gaslight you to thinking that there's no problems". Here again, the misogynist language and practice of "gaslighting" that we introduced earlier in the book is used by Belle to describe the dismissal and denigration of her lived experience and knowledge of her home by her landlord. Not only had Belle been contending with the harmful power dynamics of a violent ex-partner, but now she was forced to confront a landlord who refused to honour his responsibilities to his tenant.

Furious with her landlord's response, Belle decided to stop paying the part of the rent that came out of her pocket: it felt grossly unfair to her that what little money she had should be spent on a property that was essentially unliveable. She also decided to call the local environmental health team to come and inspect the house. So started a long back-and-forth of trying to schedule appointments to fit around work and school drop-offs: "they were telling me to be available for a certain time . . . and I'm like 'I'm dropping the kids off at school at 9 o'clock!'".

Belle's experiences highlight the emotional labour and time involved in fighting poor housing conditions, especially as a sole parent of young children. Being homeless is a form of "survival work" that demands an intense amount of time and energy.[18] For homeless mothers, life can become what Silvia Federici calls "one of uninterrupted work, with no time to rest and recuperate".[19] Belle also had the added stress of a violent and coercive ex-partner regularly trying to manipulate her into getting back together or trying to bully her into agreeing that the children should live with him. One of his key methods of abuse was economic, withholding Child Maintenance payments and using her lack of money to claim she was an unfit mother and that he should have custody of the children. He also insisted that to give her even £15 a month, she must have sex with him. Belle was exhausted and frustrated and felt she was in an impossible situation. She told us she barely had any energy to enjoy quality time with her children as she struggled to keep them safe in the hazardous house.

When Belle eventually managed to get an appointment for an environmental health inspection, she was finally vindicated, as the officers agreed that the property was unfit for habitation. However, by this point she had built up rent arrears of around £1,000 because of non-payment of her part of the rent. The landlord issued court proceedings and Belle and her children were evicted in 2019. Years of living in temporary accommodation began.

Belle's story is not unusual. Laura, a White woman in her mid-forties, was also a victim of both domestic abuse and unregulated landlordism. Laura had suffered at the hands of her abusive partner for 18 years. One night, he beat her for 45 minutes in front of their daughter, Ellie. Scared that her mum would be killed, Ellie rang the police. That night was a tipping point for Laura. The assault made her fear for their lives. But another fear now the police were involved was that her children would be placed into care if she remained in the violent relationship. Laura had no choice: she had to escape, whatever the cost. She found a private rental property within her budget that was in a terrible state of disrepair, including broken windows, damp and mould. Laura knew she had to get away from her violent partner as quickly as possible so took it despite its near-unliveable condition. The landlord had promised to sort out the repairs over time once she had moved in. Laura took a deep breath and signed the contract; what choice did she have but to trust her new landlord?

Nine years passed. The landlord completed none of the repairs they'd promised. Laura's patience began to wear thin: how could her landlord care so little about the increasingly dangerous state of the house? Her kids had been through so much already, witnessing their dad abusing their mum for years. Laura felt the least they deserved was a decent home: "Nothing ever got done. So, I started holding rent payments and things like that. I know I shouldn't have done it, I did bring a bit of it on myself. But it got to the point where the ceiling was leaking down into the fuse box."

Like Belle, Laura decided that she'd had enough of her landlord's negligence and started partially withholding rent. Threats of eviction soon followed. Two years, and multiple eviction notices later, Laura was evicted on the grounds that she owed £1,500 in rent arrears. The week before Christmas, she and her four children were forced to leave and declare themselves homeless. They were placed in a hotel for a few days, and then a hostel for nine weeks, before being moved into a temporary flat for three years. Laura had ended up in the private rented sector, vulnerable to arrears and eviction, because of needing to leave a violent partner. In a failing state it is women like Belle and Laura who are the ones trying to hold their landlords to account for their violations of the right to adequate housing and the Decent Home Standard. Unscrupulous landlords again operate with impunity while mothers and their children continue to be made homeless. It's not families that are failing, families are being failed.

Judged

Following eviction from their private rented properties, many of the women we spoke with began a journey characterized by being constantly on the move, while simultaneously being left waiting for the local authority to help them. Some, like Orla, were unsure of their next move, or whether the council would help them, so resorted to sofa-surfing before eventually realizing they were out of options and approaching their local council.

The trauma of waiting is also reflected in Jade's experiences. In Chapter 3 we introduced Jade's story of family homelessness, domestic abuse and debt. The night Jade left her abusive partner, she and her kids went to stay on a friend's sofa. When she went to the council a few days later to tell them she was homeless, Jade was asked if she could stay with friends and family for a while longer. Temporary accommodation would take some time to arrange. This became a pattern, where every time Jade went to the council offices, she was encouraged to keep sofa-surfing for the "time being". Eventually, she made the decision to go and stay with her nan, who lives in the southeast of England, until the council could find her something:

> So, what I did before we went in temporary accommodation I was living with friends, family on sofas, whatever. And they kept telling me every time I went in [to the council office], they kept saying to me, can you stay somewhere else for a bit longer? So come to Christmas time, I said right, I can go and stay with my Nan in Essex. So . . . I went to stay with my Nan . . . and they sent me a letter when I was there. For an appointment. So when I came back, I came back the day before the kids was back in school. I came back and they've cancelled all my applications because I didn't attend the appointment. So we had to start all over again.

Despite the council delaying their statutory duty to house her, it was Jade who was penalized and made to wait longer for temporary accommodation to be arranged. This, too, was the case for Zofia, who we introduced earlier in the book. She had needed to hide from her violent ex-partner and had been moved several times across the country to various women's refuges. Zofia told us she was often put to the back of the queue for temporary accommodation and told that she was not entitled to benefits, all because she was given no choice but to move from pillar to post to escape her abuser and keep safe.

In Chapter 3 we recounted how, after eventually building up the courage to go to her local council for help after fleeing her violent partner, Jade was dismissed as a liar because she hadn't gone to the police. Women we spoke with often found institutional spaces such as council offices and police stations to be sites of trauma and despair rather than spaces of recognition, support or hope. After Jade became homeless, she sat in the council offices yet again, terrified, in suspense about whether she would be offered anywhere for her and her kids to stay, or whether she would yet again be scrambling to find a friend with room on their sofa for another night or two.

The council employee's previous total dismissal of her experiences of domestic abuse, and flippant attitude towards her and her children's long-term sofa-surfing, had left Jade feeling drained and uncertain about what was going to happen next. People-watching to distract herself while she waited to be seen, she saw a commotion at one of the desks. A council employee was insisting that the man at her counter did not have dirty enough hands to be homeless: "they turned him away because his hands weren't dirty enough. They were not even listening [to him], not interested. 'You're hands aren't dirty so you've obviously got somewhere to stay'." Jade looked on, stunned, as the man grew increasingly irate. The incident ended with him being rugby tackled to the ground before being thrown out of the building. All because it's apparently impossible for someone who is homeless to have clean hands. Jade gulped, looking down at her own hands. What would her fate be? Did she look "homeless enough" to get a roof over her kids' heads tonight?

Jade shared this experience at a project feedback session we held at the Greater Manchester baby bank in late 2023. Her story was met with anger by other participants, both at how she and the man described had been treated by the council employee, but also at how much the story resonated with their own experiences. They too had suffered being judged. Several women recounted stories of being accused by council employees of lying about their homelessness status. These accusations were often based on assumptions around their appearance, and not looking "believably homeless". Taniyah and Zofia both shared stories of going to the council to declare themselves homeless, dressing nicely to present themselves as respectable people, only to be told that they didn't look unkempt enough to be in genuine need. Either way, women cannot win:

> Taniyah: If they don't believe you, your story, they insult you and say that you're gonna break [under their interrogation] because you're lying to them for some reason.
>
> Zofia: Me, me, the same. They look on me, you know, because I put my lashes on or something and they straight away, you know, ah ha [judgemental tone].
>
> Taniyah: Like, yeah, you don't need help, clearly. Why would you say that? I put on my own lash. Yeah. Really. I dig on my eyes a couple times trying to get it on to look cute. Yeah, and she didn't even give me

> a chance. She said, I don't believe your story. I'm like, what story, I'm telling you the truth.

Zofia's and Taniyah's experiences are laden with gendered undertones: the assumption being that if they can spend money on false lashes and turn up in a nice outfit, then they must be attempting to game the system. Their stories speak to long-standing tropes, particularly in relation to single mothers, of women manipulating their way to welfare access. In the US, the term "welfare queen" is often used to disparagingly describe African American single mothers in receipt of benefits, the overt assumption being that these women have chosen to have children for the express purpose of accessing state housing and benefits.[20] In previous research with families experiencing homelessness in Dublin, Ireland, we found similar tropes being wielded against them. Some housing officers and other support staff we spoke to suggested getting pregnant was a well-known fast track route onto high-priority housing waiting lists.[21] The proliferation of such depictions of single mothers highlights that the experience of homelessness is gendered not only in relation to issues such as domestic abuse and financial coercion but also in how women who attempt to access help and support from state institutions are disbelieved and dismissed as manipulators and system gamers.

Denial of women's experiences by the state were also extremely racialized. Again, the council office was implicated as a harmful site of racial abuse and trauma. This was especially acute for Taniyah. She is from a Caribbean British Overseas Territory, and therefore a British citizen. And yet, Taniyah experienced overwhelming racist abuse by council staff who not only disbelieved her citizenship status – despite the passport in her hand – but also unabashedly hurled her with racial slurs. As she describes:

> I was called a "whore n****r ". I was like, OK, wow. A Council member of staff... They threatened to take my kids. They sent me to this lady at child services and [she told me] since you are new to the country we've got nothing to offer you. Here's a ticket, so you can go back home. I'm like "sweethearts, let me explain something to you guys". At this point. I'm upset. I am British. This is my passport. Yes. OK. It's not the blue one, because my passport hasn't expired.[22] I am British.

> I wasn't born in the UK, but I fall under the UK colony. So stop it. She said, "but you have an accent". I say "yes, I do have an accent. My family is from the Caribbean. I'm from the Caribbean. But I do have rights. Yeah, and you're being very disrespectful. How would you feel if I call you a cracker?"[23] She's like, "see this disrespectfulness I'm going to call security". I said "I don't care. You need to help me." She's like "n****r, you need to stay where you came from". They don't help you. They insult you before they help you.

Taniyah worked hard to stay composed through these various encounters. She was aware of the racist stereotype of the "angry Black woman", which she went to additional lengths to counter. Like other Black women facing systematic racism, she was being compelled to use "effortful coping styles" that, according to psychologist Briana Brownlow, involve "emotional suppression, hypervigilance for threat, and high distress tolerance, which bear close analogy to coping styles frequently used among individuals facing chronic racial stress".[24] Other women of colour we met, such as Namono, who was originally from Uganda, experienced racism in temporary accommodation from other women. Upon becoming homeless, she moved into a hotel for eight days before shifting between two other communal forms of temporary accommodation. In one of these, where she stayed for several months, Namono experienced racism from several White mothers and her daughter wasn't welcomed to play with their children, no matter how polite and unassuming Namono tried to be. Temporary accommodation can be isolating, traumatic and reminiscent of a prison-like existence that women are desperate to leave.

Taniyah had hoped that her calm approach would be positively received. However, this controlled approach was met with negative commentary and suspicion of an ulterior motive, with one council worker responding to Taniyah's unflustered demeanour by telling her that "I cannot cope with you, with all your nonchalance". Taniyah's experience is indicative of the extreme level of prejudice often experienced by a group of people who are in an already incredibly vulnerable position, and how discrimination relating to gender, race, ethnicity and country of origin intersect and compound to further entrap women faced with homelessness in an impossible position. There is an expectation placed upon those presenting to their local authority as homeless to prove the validity of their experiences and remain grateful for any help they receive, even as they are potentially disbelieved, and in the worst cases, lambasted with abuse:

> Jade: You're in a predicament, where you've got to keep your mouth shut, because otherwise they're not going to [help you].
>
> Lucy: It's like we're put in a worse situation than we were originally in.

It took many of the women we spoke with weeks after they had been evicted or forced to flee domestic abuse before they were offered temporary accommodation. In the meantime, they were often stuck in unsuitable conditions, moving themselves and their children from friend's sofa to friend's sofa, with little sense of how long this would go on for. Although being eventually placed into temporary accommodation felt like a step forward at first, for many their rent arrears continued to haunt – and trap – them. As Belle, Laura, Jessica and others were to later discover, rent arrears are a double-edged form of debt. Going into rent arrears, either through withholding rent in protest at the quality of their housing or being unable to pay the rent itself, not only pushed these mothers into homelessness but also went on to prevent them and their children from escaping their rent arrears.

Debt trapped by housing allocation policies

Most councils in England have housing-related debt rules in their housing allocation policies. Our research found that 88 per cent have an ineligibility policy linked to housing-related debt and 54 per cent have a deprioritization policy linked to housing-related debt. Ineligibility and deprioritization relates to a housing register and bidding process that most English local authorities use to allocate social housing. Our research shows that in December 2023 alone, 3,797 households in temporary accommodation had been determined as ineligible for social housing owing to rental arrears. This is almost certainly a significant underestimate, and we believe the true figure to be upwards of 10,000 households across England. Forty-three per cent of these households – nearly half – include at least one child under the age of

18 and 5 per cent of these households include a child who is two years old or under. Hundreds of households in temporary accommodation are also being deprioritized from social housing because of rent arrears. Over half of these households (51 per cent) include at least one child under the age of 18, and 14 per cent of households include a child who is two years old or under.[25]

London is at the epicentre of these harsh rules. In the dataset, London is a hotspot for the numbers of households impacted by debt ineligibility rules: 79 per cent of ineligible households living in temporary accommodation reside in a London Borough; 44 per cent of these households – nearly one in two – include at least one child under the age of 18 and 4 per cent of these households include a child who is two years old or under. These findings reveal the punitive impact of family homelessness and debt on children, made concrete through the abstract architectures of housing allocation policies. Yet the numbers of households with dependent children who have been impacted by housing-related debt rules in the capital are likely to be a gross underestimate. This is because of the many boroughs that failed to reply with figures. "Numbers and justice have long kept company, as the paired words counting and accounting attest. If you can *count* something, you can also *account* for it", Sheila Jasanoff writes.[26] The lack of counting by councils, and the inability – refusal even – to count households in response to our Freedom of Information (FOI) request, attests to the continued challenge of holding power to *account* for policies inflicting harm.

There appears to be little focus on these problematic rules, and this is itself a problem. Our goal is that they do become subject to greater scrutiny and action so that indebted homeless families are not punished for housing-related debts accrued due to circumstances that are partly or wholly out of their control. We are aware, however, of the uphill struggle that overturning these rules will probably entail, given the judgements made about potential tenants on the basis of housing-related debt. Some councils, for example, describe households in rent arrears as "unsuitable tenants" and class them as "guilty of unacceptable behaviour" alongside antisocial behaviour. Most policies in England embed moralistic conceptions of debt that deny debtors access to not just housing but also the possibility for compassion. Such policy formation is tantamount to state-endorsed stigma that is designed to apportion blame solely to those who owe financial debt.

More punitive local authorities limit discretion, exemptions and "exceptional" or "mitigating" circumstances in relation to their allocation policies. On exemptions, we discovered that although 94 per cent of council policies mention domestic abuse in their housing allocation policies, only 17 per cent specifically state that they exempt victims from housing-related debt rules. There is commonly, too, a deeply problematic equivalence drawn under "unacceptable behaviour": for example, "significant housing-related debt" and "being a perpetrator of domestic abuse" are sometimes listed together in housing allocation policies as grounds for exclusion. The grouping of domestic abuse perpetrators with debtors (who may well be survivors of domestic abuse) is an act of bureaucratic and patriarchal violence. Policy inscriptions such as these manufacture a simplistic and entirely erroneous conflation between them.

We maintain, too, that housing allocation policies can work to obscure and absolve state complicity for household debts accrued. Councils are complicit in this. These rules are hard barriers to overcome. Support workers in Greater Manchester we interviewed acknowledged that repaying housing-related debt was very difficult for people in high levels of debt and with little or no income: "some people are just trapped in that situation. That [rent arrears] can take years to pay off." Families are being left in limbo in temporary accommodation, where new forms of debt can easily accrue and compound the old.

Belle was not aware of her local authority's housing allocation policy at the time, but her decision to withhold rent payments in protest at the landlord's failings resulted in not only her eviction and homelessness but also her becoming stuck for several years in temporary accommodation. The rent arrears under this tenancy rendered her ineligible to bid for permanent social housing. At the time of writing, Belle and her five children remain in temporary accommodation. Although she has worked hard to pay off the majority of one set of her rent arrears, her debts are still over £1,000, which means she remains ineligible to bid for social housing. She is considering re-entering the private rental market so she can leave temporary accommodation, but she worries this is not realistic given rising prices in the private sector. Belle and her family have little option but to continue living in temporary accommodation because of a combination of rent arrears and unaffordability of alternatives.

After being evicted by her landlady because of her growing rent arrears, Jessica and her son Archie were housed by the council in temporary accommodation. This consisted of a bedroom with a private toilet and shower room and a communal kitchen area. Jessica hated it there. The kitchen was always filthy, and there were constantly problems with other residents using drugs and getting into fights in the communal areas. Jessica was so afraid of her new-found surroundings that she often kept Archie in their room all day, including on school days, because she was so scared of him being attacked as they walked through the building. Eventually, after six long months, they were moved into accommodation that was cleaner and calmer, although they still had to share kitchen and bathroom facilities with many other people. Jessica worried about the impact of regular moves and a lack of privacy on Archie's well-being. Additionally, the logistics of getting him to school were stressful as they'd been moved away from her local area. He was also about to start secondary school, and Jessica wanted him to go to the same school as his friends so that he might have some stability and normalcy. On that basis, Jessica asked her mum if Archie could move in with her; to her relief, her mum agreed.

While Archie now lives with his grandmother permanently, Jessica has resorted to a life of sofa-surfing, sometimes at her mum's, sometimes staying with friends. She doesn't see how this situation is going to end. Because of her rent arrears, she is unable to bid on social housing: "it's just hard, like even now I still can't pay anything off. I'm still living day to day." She has considered trying to rent privately again but the rents are now far outside of Jessica's budget. Jessica is desperate for her and Archie to be together, have some security and start to build a home. Her debts weigh on her, preventing her from making any inroads into her future. She wants to deal with the debts but doesn't know where to start, and every time she thinks about it, she just wants to get into bed and stay there. Jessica has had appointments with a local debt relief charity, who advised her to make a list of everything she owes, but she finds the thought of this completely overwhelming, and she isn't even sure where half of that information would be. Indebtedness seeps into every aspect of day-to-day life, characterized by a permanent state of heightened anxiety.[27] For Jessica, being trapped in long-term homelessness because of her debts has left her feeling helpless and worthless, and with the sense that there is nothing much that can be done to alter her situation: "I feel when I do get support... it's just the minimum, it's not much. They look at me and don't know what to do ... I just feel like I'm a pest if I ask the council to help me out... It doesn't feel good. [I feel] ... so closed off now, so like my personality is different, I'm not the same person."

For Jessica, rent arrears not only forced her into homelessness, they have also trapped her in homelessness. She has been stripped of her confidence and her sense of self-worth. Jessica now carries with her deep mistrust: that the local authority and support organizations, at best, can't do anything to help her, and at worst, see her as a nuisance and undeserving of a decent home. Mistrust hardened for women as they discovered that institutions apparently there to support them, were actually undermining them. After being made homeless and living in temporary accommodation for two years, Laura discovered that the managers of her former private rental home had incorrectly calculated her rent arrears:

> But while all this moving about was going on, it turned out that I didn't actually owe £1,500 rent arrears, my property managers were holding some of the rent payments saying that they hadn't received it. And it was because of the eviction housing benefit had looked into the claim properly. And it turned out that there were three payments missing. And it took me a month to get the revised rent statement... as showing these missing payments. So, these three payments hadn't been put on to this rent arrears that I owe. Anyway, it turned out that I only owed £400 and something pounds in arrears. So, I was falsely evicted.

If the arrears had been correctly calculated, Laura believes her landlord would have been less likely to evict her, or that the court order would have been less likely to be successful. This means that she was potentially forced into homelessness and the temporary accommodation system unnecessarily, through no fault of her own. Even if Laura was incorrect in her assumption, and her landlord would have ensured she was evicted regardless of the sum owed, she had spent two years unable to bid for social housing because of the misreported size of her arrears. Laura and her children had spent two years stuck in temporary accommodation, not so much because of debt, but because of mismanaged bureaucracy in a failing state.

Imprisoned in debt

Perched together on the sofa listening, Orla told us that she wonders how she'll ever get out of temporary accommodation. With the help of a local charity support worker, Orla has managed to clear enough of her rent arrears to begin the social housing bidding process, but new problems have appeared. In part because she's been paying off these debts, she hasn't been able to afford her council tax and other bills: the post box we mentioned earlier in the chapter was stuffed full of payment demands. Orla believes these arrears run into the thousands. She told us some of them are red letters: the scary ones. But she just can't face opening them. It's all become too much. As we explained in Chapter 1, even if Orla paid off some of the council tax arrears, local authorities often mandate residents to repay the full outstanding balance of the annual bill or else to be summoned to court. She is unable to keep up with one payment, let alone pay for a full year. Orla explained how she cannot afford childcare costs and has no family support, so getting back to work feels impossible for now. How on earth are mothers meant to cope with all of this under such challenging and intractable circumstances?

Debt is a key trigger for women's entry into homelessness and temporary accommodation, and it is one over which they have little control. The Renters' Rights Bill, for example, does not tackle the unaffordability of the private rented sector and offers little hope for vulnerable households struggling with rental arrears. Orla's experiences illustrate that debt not only unhomes families and casts them into temporary accommodation but also works against their rehoming and keeps them stuck there. Despite being some of the most vulnerable and in need of housing security, mothers are held back from the opportunity to access long-term affordable housing. This is in part because of housing allocation policies that lack nuance and compassion. Many of the women we met were initially in debt because they had been economically abused by former partners, but they were now also victims of institutional systems that penalized them because of this.

Given the widespread presence of rent arrears and debt in housing allocation policies, it is critical to ask: are housing-related debt rules excluding those most in need of housing? Our answer? A resounding yes. The CIH has raised more general concerns in this regard, concerning "decisions about who gets access to waiting lists, how those who do get access are prioritized and the potential for pre-tenancy activity to exclude those most in need of social housing". The CIH exists, as per their mission statement, "to support housing professionals to create a future in which everyone has a place to call home". Their *Rethinking Allocations* report is clear that ensuring tenancies are sustainable is important, "but activity to help achieve this is undermining efforts to house those who need homes the most".[28] As Alison's testimony revealed at the start of this chapter, it is hardly surprising that underresourced and overpressured local authorities and their staff are resorting to "rationing" in an "absolutely broken system". Single mothers' experiences combined with the national-level data we collected demonstrates how housing allocation policies are working against families' best interests in twenty-first century England. Households in temporary accommodation are being judged as financial risks as tenants rather than as vulnerable families with children who need housing. Their access to housing is being "rationed" on the numerical basis of debts against their name.

The state is, in effect, incarcerating homeless indebted mothers and their children in temporary accommodation until housing shortages ease and the need for rationing can be revoked. But families cannot wait for this. Entire childhoods are being rationed. Temporary accommodation is the debtors' prison of the contemporary era, which, like those preceding it in the eighteenth and early nineteenth centuries in England, can involve whole families cramped in overcrowded and damp conditions. In Chapter 5, the human impacts of being imprisoned for debt in temporary accommodation come into full and horrifying view.

SAM

IKEA "Real Life Roomset" [in collaboration with Shelter] March 2023 visit, Hammersmith, London

Homeless after her relationship broke down, Sam and her three young children were placed in a hostel room like this. Concerned about her safety, she moved out, sleeping in a car for seven weeks while her children stayed with a friend.

Finally, she was given new accommodation which was no better than the first. There was black mould everywhere and a lingering smell of cannabis. There was a hole in the door where the letterbox should have been, and on two occasions, she was assaulted while living there. Worst of all, Sam was separated from her three children yet again because her temporary accommodation was an hour and 40 minutes away from their school. The constant upheavals and separation tested the resilience of the family.

Thousands of families are stuck in places like this because they have nowhere else to go. IKEA have joined forces with Shelter to highlight this issue and call on the government to build 90,000 new social homes a year. By 2030, our aim is to ensure that half-a-million people have access to a better life at home.[29]

*

YOU NEED
TO
PACK UP
YOUR
WHOLE
LIFE
WITHIN
6
HOURS

5

Family lives caught in costly limbo

The human costs of living in temporary accommodation are the focus of this chapter. Families are caught and imprisoned in a limbo that is fundamentally antithetical to their happiness, health and life chances. As London councils recognize,[1] having "secure and stable housing is fundamental for accessing opportunity and maintaining wellbeing", yet the reality of what is transpiring deviates so far from this ideal that it constitutes a "national emergency". In 2023 a collaboration was born from this emergency, between the housing charity Shelter and IKEA UK. The organizations teamed up to design a "Real Life Roomset", to be displayed in IKEA stores. Hiliary Jenkins, sustainability business partner at IKEA and Ireland, explained to us why they chose to recreate temporary accommodation in four of their English stores:

> Hidden homelessness is in fact hidden, people don't realise that there are homeless children in this country, and we came together [with Shelter] to have an honest conversation about what we could do together to shine a light on what is a very hidden emergency ... Obviously at IKEA we believe that home is the most important place on earth, and Shelter has that same vision.[2]

The roomsets bring family homelessness "out of the closet", aiming to offer customers a disturbing visualization of this emergency. They are part of Shelter and IKEA UK's collective call for the government to build more social homes. We visited the Swedish brand's inner-city Hammersmith store in London to take a closer look. While smaller than its more suburban counterparts, the store included the usual inspirational roomsets that bring its furniture, textiles, lighting and home decor "alive". Trying to find the roomset involved, much like shopping in IKEA, fighting off distraction and a rising sense of confusion. The ground-floor entry level was chock-a-block with thousands of products: candles, cushions, cooking utensils, and more. Going down the escalator to the basement, we first hit the kitchen showroom area. A light box read, "Your space to escape city life" (Figure 5.1). Turning left, we were greeted by the design area where customers can start planning "The island of your dreams". To make this dream happen, one of IKEAs posters provides the answer: up to £15,000 of credit (Figure 5.2).

Figure 5.1 "Your space to escape city life"

Source: Photo by K. Brickell, March 2023.

Past the credit advertisement was a warren of roomsets. Opposite a lounge with a lightbox quoting "A door to a place we call home" was the "Real Life Roomset" (Figure 5.3). On the outer wall a poster asked, "Could you live here?" Sam's story and that of her three children hung from the entrance.[3]

Figure 5.2 Credit advertisement

Source: Photo by K. Brickell, March 2023.

Figure 5.3 Sam's IKEA "Real Life Roomset" in Hammersmith

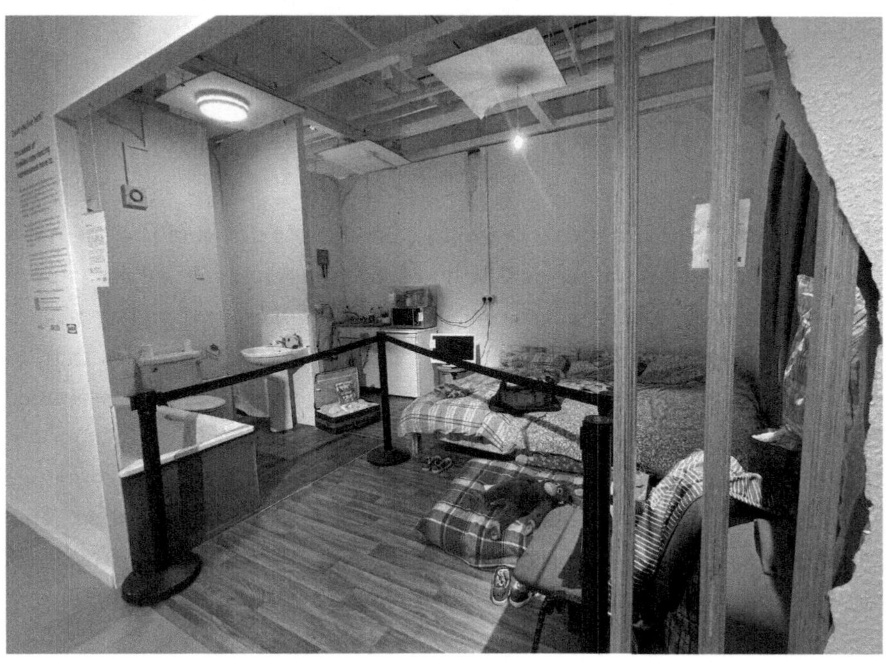

Source: Photo by K. Brickell, March 2023.

The setup showed a family's life in one room. Ripped wallpaper, damp stains, lingering mould, cockroach stoppers and surface-mounted electrics. Beds so tightly pushed together and in such a small space that walking into the room almost caused us to trip and fall onto a child's mattress laid on the floor. Battery-powered lights twinkling, willing an inkling of home. Colouring pens strewn, school uniform ready, a toiletry bag perched on the sink. Play, learning and well-being thrown but attempted. The rest of a family's belongings banished to bags and suitcases of the displaced not holidayed. Life lived in limbo.

Our point of departure for this chapter then is the growing inequality of life chances told through the home and the credit–debt relations through which it is made and unmade. The island-kitchened, homeowning middle-class England, and the kitchenless forced to live in temporary accommodation without so much as a stove. From the cramped spaces of temporary accommodation to experiences of moving between them, and typically at speed, this chapter reveals lives in limbo. It delves into the negative financial and other impacts of this limbo through the experiences of Jade, Beatrix, Namono and Casho from Greater Manchester and Stephanie and Elizabeth from London. Collectively their stories show their imprisonment in temporary accommodation as the breeding ground for the building of debt, trauma, ill-health and risks to life itself.

Confined

For some mothers in England their baby's life outside the womb began in the confines of a small hotel room. The hotel that most families we met stayed in is described by online guest reviews as having damaged plaster from a roof leak, being unclean and having rain coming through windows that do not shut properly. After sofa-surfing for a year and then seeking assistance from the council, Jade (who we met in Chapter 4) and her two children moved into a room in this hotel. There was no space for their belongings and their stuff began to accumulate over the five months of living there. This impacted her children's ability to move around and play. Health researchers have found that for under fives living in temporary accommodation during the Covid-19 pandemic, delay and regression in developmental milestones and behaviours (such as toileting, feeding skills, emotional regulation and social-communication skills) worsened.[4] In our own pre-pandemic research in Dublin, Ireland, mothers self-reported this too. Una, for example, was told by an early intervention team that the developmental delay of her son was probably because of the limited space in the hotel room the family of three shared: "He has to see the early intervention team, because he can't climb or walk stairs and he was kind of a rigid baby. They're [the specialists] convinced now that it's down to where we lived, because he hadn't got access to like move around, to crawl, he never crawled ... he had no space at all like."[5]

For Jade and many other families we met in England, such risks to children's development and health were accompanied by the everyday travails of social reproductive work in a hotel. Laundry was expensive – £3 per wash – so with her children Jade had to regularly lug the washing to her nan's. Storing milk for her baby daughter was a challenge with no fridge provided or allowed. A microwave for heating up milk and food was also out of the question. The Magpie Project, a London-based charity focused on helping mums and pre-school children in temporary and insecure accommodation, have campaigned for kitchens to be provided in all temporary accommodation. Like Jade, the mothers they work with have reported struggling to sterilize bottles, make up baby feeds and prepare or afford the foods needed for weaning.[6] The Magpie Project campaign asks those in power and those who might sign their petition to imagine what it is like to live without a kitchen (Figure 5.4).

The Magpie Project argue that in "the sixth largest economy in the world, it is unnecessary and unacceptable that children's health and long-term development is being put at risk by the lack of basic facilities".[7] They propose a total ban on the use of hotels that do not have kitchens for families with children under five. Further to this, they advocate for local authority housing departments to be given the resources to ensure that no family has to live in a hotel without a kitchen for more than six weeks, and that in the meantime, national government support families through food vouchers, community kitchens and – where possible – rings, hobs or microwaves in their rooms.

Figure 5.4 Campaign postcard by The Magpie Project, 2024

Source: courtesy of The Magpie Project.

At the charity Justlife's 2023 Temporary Accommodation Conference in Westminster, community child health scholar and practitioner Monica Lakhanpaul outlined the adverse impacts of growing up in temporary accommodation with its many space and kitchen facility limitations: "How does the child see the world in those four walls, where they can't walk around because there's no space for them, where they can't develop their bones, where they get vitamin D deficiency because there's no sunlight coming in, where they are iron deficient because there is no food to eat?"[8]

Without a kitchen, the families we met had no means to make food in hotel rooms and they were forced to eat out and consume takeaway meals. Mothers felt their health and that of their children was worsening. Added to this, their limited finances were being further drained by the high costs of eating outside the home. Homeless families don't have IKEA kitchens "to escape city life". Instead, they are kitchenless and without the money to feed their families adequately. Namono, who we meet later in the chapter, found this, "Because while you're there, you only have a kettle. You don't even have a microwave or anything, and you have to buy food . . . everything was just quite expensive really."

A staff member of the charity who supported homeless women in Greater Manchester highlighted that the location of the local hotel that most of their families stay in creates ripe conditions for exacerbating hardship: "You're in what we call a food desert because where the hotel is, you can't get to Aldi. You know, just look at your local supermarket and then look at a corner shop, see the difference in price."

Here the higher prices that smaller convenience shops tend to charge in comparison with large supermarkets is alluded to. "Food deserts" are a form of geography-based disadvantage linked to poor social or health outcomes from not having access to healthy, affordable food. In Britain there are estimated to be 10.2 million individuals living in food deserts.[9] A Sky News report on the "food desert" phenomenon starts: "If you want to know what food insecurity looks like, it's a queue of people waiting in the drizzle outside an Oldham community centre for fresh food they can't otherwise afford."[10]

The Trussell Trust food bank in Oldham, Greater Manchester, was described by our research participants as a "lifeline" during stays in temporary accommodation.[11] Reliance on food banks cannot be overstated, with Oldham's Inclusion and Support team stating to us that food bank referrals are a major part of their helpline service to the extent that "food banks are running out . . . where do you go from there?" In August 2023, the food bank had already supported over 15,000 people, 6,000 more than the same period in 2022. Donations however have fallen as more people who may have donated have come under financial stress themselves. The food bank is increasingly eating into its own funds to purchase items. A volunteer commented on the speed that the food leaves the building, and that the food bank's clients have "got nothing and it's 2023 in England. It's unbelievable."[12]

Food banks have become increasingly essential for families in poverty in England. Single parents who are in problem debt experience this acutely as they try to square feeding their families and making debt repayments. According to a large-scale survey of 3,796 adults across England and Wales,

66 per cent of single parents had to cut back on food for themselves as a result of making debt repayments; 20 per cent of single parents had to cut back on food for their children; and 19 per cent of single parents in problem debt had recently used a food bank, compared to 12 per cent of those not in problem debt.[13] Children are paying the price for the debt trap in their empty stomachs and compromised health and well-being. They are victims of cutbacks in the most vital and visceral of ways that will negatively reverberate into their futures as adults.

Deadly

While families caught in cramped temporary accommodation commonly find their health and well-being eroded through the lack of kitchen facilities and space for children to play, they can also face other forms of deficient provision, spatial constraints and unsafe conditions. At times these can prove deadly. Sitting in the packed auditorium at a 2023 Justlife event in Westminster, this uncomfortable truth was laid bare. Sam Pratt, Shared Health Foundation's policy and communications lead, made his way to the podium with a box. Without explaining why and immediately launching into his talk about conditions in temporary accommodation, he began pulling out sets of babies' and children's shoes from the box (Figure 5.5), slowly and steadily placing them on the lectern.

Shifting awkwardly in our seats as audience members, we learned at the end of his talk that the number of pairs of shoes precariously piled up through his speech was communicating a grave finding. The Child Death Overview Panel of the National Child Mortality Database discovered that 55 child deaths between 2019 to 2023 list temporary accommodation as a contributing factor to the child's vulnerability, ill-health and death.[14] Forty-two of these children were under one year old and 22 of them from ethnic minority backgrounds. The figures for 2023–4 show 80 child deaths in temporary accommodation, accounting for 3 per cent of the total number of child deaths during this period.[15] These are avoidable child deaths steeped in racism and the failure of the state to protect the lives of all children. The heightened dangers for children in temporary accommodation are multiple.

Figure 5.5 Box with pairs of babies' shoes to represent their deaths in temporary accommodation

Source: Photo by K. Brickell, September 2023.

First, hotel and B&B rooms do not always ensure a safe place, and enough space, for children to sleep. While most media and government attention has focused on the "rough sleeping" of single adults, homeless children's sleeping has been grossly neglected in comparison. The APPG for Households in Temporary Accommodation have raised the alarm on the increased risks of sudden infant death syndrome (SIDS) for thousands of homeless children.[16] In his talk at the Justlife event, Sam revealed how the non-standard provision of cots, combined with scarcity of space for a full-size cot, is elevating risks of child death by forcing families to bed share, resulting in hazardous co-sleeping. In respect to space, the overcrowding section of the 1985 Housing Act does not count babies up to age one in its protections. "The space standard" is "contravened" in the Act "when the number of persons sleeping in a dwelling is in excess of the permitted number, having regard to the number and floor area of the rooms of the dwelling available as sleeping accommodation". Yet clause 362/2a delimits that "for this purpose", "no account shall be taken of a child under the age of one". As a piece of constituency casework in the House of Commons Library asserts: "A child below the age of one is disregarded and a child between the age of one and ten counts as a half person."[17] Again, there is a sense of children's rights, including their rights to space, being coldly disregarded on technical grounds. A homeless baby's life is not being *counted*, and thus *accounted* for, by the state. Rather, the very youngest in society are being *discounted* in their spatial rights to life itself.

In the case of vulnerability related to a lack of cot provision, up until February 2024 guidance on temporary accommodation had not included cot provision, meaning that babies were even more exposed to unsafe sleeping arrangements. Shared Health Foundation lobbying changed this. The national Homelessness Code of Guidance was updated in March 2024 to include the provision of cots for children under two in temporary accommodation. England-wide research we conducted on cots and safer-sleeping advice showed that in 2023, more than 3,000 individuals were pregnant when placed in temporary accommodation. Most of our FOI requests were sent *after* the February 2024 change, with a sizeable number of local authorities reporting that they were still reviewing what this meant in practice.

Half of local authorities said they provide cots, yet even these regularly cited caveats, for example: "Yes if requested, and available", "In some cases, yes – dependant on the provider" and, "Although the Council could assist with this, it has never been needed". Our FOI research additionally found that only one in five (18 per cent) of local authorities in England provide safer sleep advice to families in temporary accommodation. Lullaby Trust safer-sleeping advice recommends, for example, that the cot is clear of items (such as toys) and that a comfortable temperature is maintained: both things that can be difficult to follow in the confines of a hotel room.[18] In response to our FOI request, which was specific to temporary accommodation, a range of reasons were also communicated for why safer sleep advice was not always given: that it was "not routine practice"; and in a few instances that it was inappropriate to do so. "No. As a landlord it would not be appropriate to advise a tenant on how to furnish the space they are placed in or give parenting advice." To put the new Homelessness Code of Guidance on cot provision into full and effective practice – and to ensure that safer-sleeping advice is consistently and effectively given – will need further pushing, as will the reasons for why safer-sleeping advice is not being given out as standard.

A second dimension of risk to children in temporary accommodation is the presence and harmful impacts of mould and damp. In response to the statistics on child deaths in temporary accommodation, The Magpie Project's director reflected on these realities in the London Borough of Newham.

> We see so many health problems in our children including delayed rolling and crawling, malnutrition and gastro-intestinal issues around lack of kitchen facilities, accidents in the home due to unsafe accommodation, bed bugs, scabies, bites by rats, and many, many incidences of respiratory distress and disease due to mould, damp and poor air quality.[19]

Such conditions and their fatal impact are captured in the Amnesty International "Before Our Eyes" campaign. Taking the form of a drama trailer, Before Our Eyes tells the story of a sole parent, Anna, who has been placed in temporary accommodation with her baby daughter.[20] Her baby has breathing difficulties and eventually dies because of the conditions they have been placed in. Mould blooms across the damp turquoise walls enclosing them. Anna had previously complained to the council about the conditions, urging the local authority housing officer (played by Adrian Lester) to move them: "I cannot stay here, it's making her sick." The response was to say she is on the waiting list; there was nothing else to be done. Soon after her baby's death, Anna reaches out to a lawyer (played by Olivia Colman) for help to seek justice as the local authority denied all responsibility for her baby's death. They take the local authority to court, albeit after the housing officer tries to dissuade them. He reveals: "I care about these kids. I was one of them. But it doesn't matter, it doesn't matter if people like you care about them. Until their lives matter to society, they're invisible." The gritty and tear-inducing trailer links to the feminist political theorist Judith Butler's idea of grievable life: that for a person to be viewed worthy of mourning, they must be first recognized as a life, something that is conditional on how that life is framed.[21] We have seen conditionality befall the treatment of Grenfell Tower residents before and after the 2017 fire which killed 72 people, including 18 children, and here in the Amnesty International campaign when it comes to the acute and ongoing risks posed to children's lives in temporary accommodation. The fact that in overcrowding legislation children aged between one and ten years old are only technically recognized as 0.5 of a person is reflective of how they are not seen as a whole life. The housing officer's words also go to the heart of the compassion deficit that characterizes English society, where a culture of blame persists and is apportioned out to "failing families" rather than to the failings of the nation to support, care and value the lives of all.

The Amnesty International trailer then moves to a courtroom scene, where Anna takes a stand at the dock. She begins, "I know what you think when you look at me. She must have done something wrong. I ticked all the boxes. I tried to do everything right. It wasn't enough." Anna's speech is wrought with the idea of her (and mothers like her) having failed, despite going to huge lengths to try and provide a safe home for her baby daughter. The trailer is a powerful critique of guilt applied to and by Anna, and underscores our own contention that it is not women who have failed, it is women who have been failed.

At the end of the trailer, a member of the production staff calls out, "and cut", and Olivia Colman reveals: "This isn't drama. This is real life." Amnesty International reflect on what their "drama" means in relation to human rights at risk in the UK:

> Right here at home, a chilling reality is unravelling – millions of families cannot access the basic human rights they need to live; from safe shelter to access to healthcare, food and more. This crisis does not come from a lack of resources, as we are often led to believe. It comes from economic and social inequality, which is felt by many across the country.[22]

In England the fundamental human rights of women and children are being infringed on a daily and systematic basis. This can be described as no less than a failing state. As we learned in Chapter 4, the Renters' Rights Bill marks the introduction of a Decent Homes Standard to the private rented sector. Temporary accommodation was, despite a proposed amendment to include it in the Bill, initially excluded. In October 2024, we listened to newly elected Labour MP Danny Beale, who himself had experience of homelessness as a child, explain why temporary accommodation could not be included under the Decent Home Standard. If it was, he told the room, there wouldn't be enough supply to match demand. In other words, too much of the temporary accommodation housing stock would fail minimum standards. We sat together hearing this damning indictment at Amnesty International's HQ in London, a bitter irony given the organization's "Before Our Eyes" campaign.

In February 2025, at the charity Crisis' Homelessness Summit in central London, homelessness minister Rushanara Ali announced that Awaab's Law, which will legally require social landlords to investigate and fix dangerous damp and mould within set times frames, will be extended to include temporary accommodation.[23] While this is certainly a win for thousands of families trapped in unsafe conditions, it raises further questions about how local authorities in particular will be able to source the funds to abide by this law without being pulled into further debts themselves. As we flagged earlier in respect to the vicious pursuit of households in council tax arrears, it seems like local authorities are only turning up the punitive dial. Some local authorities translate their need for funds into brutal policies that demand unachievable payments from their most vulnerable residents. And so the debt trap tightens.

Transient

As we have established, being caught in limbo in temporary accommodation is spatially as well as temporally punitive. The protracted transience of homeless families' lives takes its toll and puts mothers and children constantly on edge. Being given notice to leave the night before a 10 am check-out time is business as usual in the temporary accommodation sector. Unlike guests staying in hotels for short leisure breaks, the duration of stays is more uncertain for homeless families. Check-out time abruptly arrives with short notice and rather than preparing your suitcase to return home, homeless families must leave for an unknown destination. These experiences are reminiscent of those explored by forced migration and displacement scholars who use the notion of "limbo" to describe the "immobilized temporariness" in which people are "in a long-lasting and intractable state of limbo".[24] The nature of dwelling like this, forced to be ready to move between temporary accommodations with little to no notice, and at the same time wait an indeterminable time for social housing, ate into women's psyches. In the discussion group we held with some of our participants in October 2023, this was striking:

> Jade: The thing is, with temporary accommodation, I could come in today, if there's an emergency or anything, I can get a phone call tomorrow saying I've got to move. I've got to get all my stuff out of that property in that moment . . . I might not be there by the morning.
>
> Laura: You've always got that worry.
>
> Taniyah: They call you at 11 am and say "you need to be out by 3 o'clock". You need to pack up your whole life. And if you need to, pick up your kids.
>
> Jade: They rung me at 9 o'clock to be out of the hotel at 10 in the morning. I had two kids, one a baby and a child that I have to get to school. And if I weren't out, I'd get charged. I'd been there for three months. I'm like, "I have no money".

A hotel is not a home. Families deserve homes, not prison-like hotels. Like Jade, Laura and Taniyah, Beatrix had become highly accustomed to living in, and being shunted between, hotels. After a relationship breakdown and the death of her grandfather and aunt who she lived with in Portugal, she migrated in 2012 with her (then) two children to join her mother and brother in London. The family went on to move to Liverpool so that her brother could train as a professional athlete. The landlord, however, did not allow an additional adult and children in the Liverpool flat, and the family were threatened with eviction. Beatrix and her children had little choice but to leave and seek support from the council. Her part-time, low-paid job in a McDonalds (around £500 per month) combined with childcare costs meant that – despite being in receipt of Working Tax Credit and Child Tax Credit – she couldn't afford the private rented sector. She was also trying to service mobile phone and catalogue debt totalling £800. Beatrix had lost a friendship recently too after being slow to repay a friend £300. The debt trap was closing in.

In the first month the family were homeless they moved between a Travelodge, a Premier Inn and a B&B. Each time it took two taxi rides to move the family's belongings, costing around £80 per move. Beatrix initially used a £27 cooking plate she bought to make food in the hotel room, but despite having the windows open the smoke alarm triggered and she was reprimanded. "And I said, but I have children." To no avail, the family was left eating fast food and spending money they didn't have after Beatrix was disallowed from using the cooking plate. After a month of ping-ponging between hotels she was placed in a temporary two-bedroom flat. While it was "better" than the hotels, there were ants everywhere, and for the duration of her three-month stay she battled them with ant powder. In 2019, Beatrix was offered a permanent maisonette flat, but her Portuguese passport had expired and with Brexit-related citizenship requirements immanent she had to travel back to Portugal to renew it. As a consequence, the offer of the flat was reneged, and after returning from the short trip to Portugal she stayed living in the ant-infested temporary flat for a further three months. By this point she was also pregnant. She panicked.

With her mother and brother having moved across the country again for his career, a friend in Greater Manchester reached out and suggested Beatrix move in with her. This didn't work out and, a few months after moving in with her friend, Beatrix was asked to leave. Again, she approached the local authority who advised her to return to Liverpool as she did not meet the local connection eligibility rules. Beatrix was adamant that her children would not move schools again. Contesting the decision, she was placed in a B&B in Manchester until a resolution was reached. The local authority concluded their review, "they said I was making myself intentionally homeless and I was putting my children at risk as well. That they had contacted social services, and the children could be housed, but I couldn't... the children would be taken away from me." According to the law (Section 191(1) of the Housing Act 2006) a person becomes homeless intentionally if all of the following apply: (1) they deliberately do or fail to do anything in consequence of which they cease to occupy accommodation; (2) the accommodation is available for their occupation; and (3) it would have been reasonable for them to continue to occupy the accommodation.[25] Given these multiple threats and the stress she was under, Beatrix moved out of the B&B and found another friend to stay with for several weeks in the city region.

Beatrix pushed the council again for help. Sofa-surfing did not offer the privacy, personal space and family routines needed. But they told her: "we don't have housing for you and we're going to take the children away because you are sofa-surfing". Kate Belgrave, a journalist who blogs on people impacted by austerity across the UK, is emphatic that such endemic intimidation must end.

> What a threat that is – and to so many people. So many people are evicted for rent arrears these days. So many women tell me that they are terrified that the council will remove their kids if they can't find decent – or any – housing for them. Getting evicted and finding yourself without a roof is bad enough. Now, homeless people believe they risk losing their kids if they return to their council to challenge an intentional homelessness decision, or if they approach a council for further housing help.
>
> This shit has to stop. Councils cannot be permitted to threaten women with the loss of their children, just because those women are poor.
>
> This situation is untenable. Let's have some #metoo outrage about it. Imagine the headlines and fury if some council tried that sort of threat on with a middle class family, or – gasp – a celeb.
>
> "We'll come after your kids." I think not.[26]

Here Belgrave raises the spectre of hypocrisy: disadvantaged women failed by an economy with spiralling housing costs being separated from their children without a modicum of outrage, versus the exposure and public fury that would ensue if this was happening to better-off families. Despite their threats against Beatrix, the council eventually placed the family in a temporary flat for three days, then an apart-hotel for one month and then another temporary flat. Several times stranded between check-out and check-in time, she breastfed her baby and hung out in the toilets of the Manchester Arndale shopping centre: "it was too stressful to just walk around, so we found this spot". After the flat the family were moved to a B&B for two nights and then back to the apart-hotel. Soon after, Beatrix and her children were moved to the *same* room in the *same* B&B they had first been placed in. Their rollercoaster lives in Greater Manchester had gone full circle. The debt trap had resulted in the family being stuck in a vicious cycle of displacement: constantly on the move, and yet going nowhere.

Ultimately relenting and accepting responsibility for the family, the local authority in Greater Manchester offered a permanent home to them in March 2023. While still under construction, Beatrix and her children waited in a temporary flat full of rat droppings. Further delay ensued as rent arrears from her previous council tenancy in Liverpool came to light. However, after showing her "intent to pay" through 12 consecutive payments, setting up a repayment plan and with the debt total hovering at £819 (under the £1,000 threshold of ineligibility), the family finally moved into the house they now call home.

Cleaned out

"I wouldn't even take someone off the street and put them in there to stay for the night." This is how Jade felt about the flat she was moved into after a hotel stay. After being evicted that morning, Jade had arrived at midday to the next temporary accommodation. She was given the keys and left alone to discover with horror an "absolutely disgusting" scene. There were "snot"-like-stains on the walls, the carpet was "crispy" in patches, "black and sludgy" in others, and the two sofas were stripped bare to the foam. The sofas "stunk like 50 people had lived there smoking fags". She recoiled: it was "soul destroying". Jade is not alone in this deep feeling of hurt from the lack of dignity and respect shown towards people experiencing homelessness through the material disrepair and dirtiness of temporary accommodation. Dirt, as British anthropologist Mary Douglas sketched in her book *Purity and Danger* in the 1960s, is "matter out of place" that connotes social classification and hierarchy.[27] Having to dwell with or deal with dirt in British society has been taken historically to symbolize a low status of housing or occupation.[28] Jade and others like Beatrix viscerally felt this, noting how they felt discarded by an uncaring state, left to live with dirt, mould, insects and vermin. They are not alone in this sentiment. The 2021 ITV television programme *Surviving Squalor: Britain's Housing Shame* brought to public view the systematic disregard for the conditions that tenants in temporary and permanent housing are enduring nationally.

Jade cried as she desperately tried to work out how to make the disgusting flat vaguely liveable for her children in the three hours she had before school and nursery pick-up. She recalled the dilemma she faced:

> I had £15 left, and I was thinking right, I could get a little bit of food, I could get some – and then I walked in and I was like, [gasps] . . . So the last £15 I had, I had to go out and buy cleaning stuff to clean the house. It was awful. It was grim . . . I bought bleach and I'm not lying, I just literally got the bottles of bleach and I just ran 'em around every wall, every side, every skirting board and left it for about an hour. And then came back in and cleaned it all.

Jade's children were again being put at risk from the temporary accommodation they were placed in, from the cramped hotel room where they were initially placed to this mould-infested flat. The health of a nation can be read through the health of its housing. By this measure, England's health is in poor shape indeed. Jade had to spend the last of that week's money on bleach rather than food – these are the "choices" mothers are faced with in England today. It is long established that a safe, secure and affordable home is foundational to leading a healthy life. Yet in a failing state this foundation is out of reach for too many.[29]

The failing state can be both injurious and deadly. In Greater Manchester, toddler Awaab Ishak died in Rochdale Boroughwide Housing from a respiratory condition caused by exposure to mould. "How in the UK in 2020 does a two-year-old child die as a result of exposure to mould?" demanded the Senior Coroner, Joanne Kearsley.[30] Awaab's parents had pleaded with the housing association for the mould be to be addressed. Their pleas had been ignored, and not only this, but after the child's death the landlord blamed "lifestyle factors" for the damp and mould, including so-called "ritual bathing" and "boiling food in pans on the stove". To depict Awaab's death as a "tragedy" then is wrong. For legal scholar Edward Kirton-Darling, this would suggest that his death was "a matter of fate, inevitable and inescapable." Rather, he died "as a result of systemic factors and individual decisions" that were preventable. Awaab's death is a sickening and indefensible indictment of a failing landlord and a failing state.[31]

When it comes to mould, the onus still remains on families to try and "make do and mend". This is in spite of the futility and danger of trying to keep mould at bay without professional assistance. Jade, for example, had been cleaned out of her final £15 by the responsibility placed on her, rather than the housing provider, to try to make the accommodation safe. Being forced to deal with the mould problem through the makeshift use of bleach did not guarantee its removal either. Spores will simply return if the source of moisture is not rectified. There was also the issue of the temporary accommodation providing no towels, bedding, crockery, cutlery or other everyday essentials. This is a stark contrast to the IKEA roomsets we visited, which were stuffed full of these necessities. Thankfully the Trussell Trust provided Jade with a "Starter Pack" that included a kettle, toaster, crockery and cutlery.

Through the 2.5 years she would go on to live in the flat, Jade got through "day by day" and "didn't make plans for anything". Like Beatrix, she was pragmatic, explaining: "The thing is, with temporary accommodation, I could come in today, if there's an emergency or anything, I can get a phone call tomorrow saying I've got to move. I've got to get all my stuff out of that property in that moment. I could come in and decorate it. I might not even be there by the morning."

For Jade, life in limbo made a folly of homemaking in any substantive way. This is not to say that she didn't make efforts to create a homely environment, or as Lucy, another mother, put it, "to feel more like home even though it's not home". In the IKEA temporary accommodation roomset, the twinkling fairy lights emitted a cosy glow, attempting a comforting sense of home in a deeply uncomfortable setting. In reality, the costs involved of buying and moving, and the temporary status of their stay, meant that investing in these "luxuries", even ones so small as fairy lights, was not an option for Jade. It was already too risky, financially and emotionally, in temporary accommodation.

Endangered

While Jade transferred into a self-contained flat after her hotel stay, some mothers' journeys took them to other forms of temporary accommodation. Some homeless families in England, for instance, find themselves in converted office blocks repurposed as temporary accommodation. It has been reported that some of these office-to-residential transitions are tantamount to "slum housing" given their structural defects, broken windows and fire doors, and damp and mould.[32] Minimum space standards are also regularly flouted. Shelter have reported that there is "further evidence that investors are purchasing office blocks, which they then convert to temporary accommodation without local authority planning permission under permitted development rights. This means there is no scope for the local planning authority to insist on national or local standards (e.g. on space)."[33]

"Deeply concerning" was the reaction that then Levelling Up Secretary Michael Gove had in 2023 to an *i News* report on the conditions that some homeless families are facing in these converted office blocks.[34] The removal of the requirement for planning permission to convert office blocks into residential buildings, and which spurred on these "slums", was premised as a clever fix in response to the 2008 global financial crisis that led to a slowdown of residential construction and a growing number of empty and derelict offices.[35] It is a "fix" that requires families to bear the harmful consequences, as buildings constructed via permitted development rights are deregulated in the planning system and many are not fit for human habitation. Similar criticisms of the Labour government are now being made as it plans to allow developers to convert office blocks into flats without controls in a bid to increase housing supply. The policy director of the Town and Country Planning Association, Hugh Ellis, has voiced his concerns: "It is shameful that

Labour has allowed this policy to continue. It is Dickensian – tolerating the creation of slum housing for those people most in need."[36]

While none of the mothers we met had lived in a converted office block, they had endured living in mixed-sex (and sometimes other repurposed) accommodation that had attendant risks, particularly for their children. This wholly unsuitable accommodation consisted of shared facilities (including shared bathrooms) and living in close proximity to adults who have mental health issues or drug and alcohol problems. The Children's Rights Alliance highlight this as major concern, and in a report on children speaking out on homelessness they cite a boy called Michael, who says: "You can't go downstairs and watch TV because there'll be someone shouting. You're locked up in one room with your family. There's nothing to do. It's like being in prison."[37]

When we brought participants together for the first time and fed our research findings back for their comment, Taniyah (who we met in Chapter 4) started a conversation about mixed accommodation too. "You should add that the temporary accommodation is sometimes unsuitable for us living in it", she urged. Lucy followed, "Yeah, they put people with children in with men – men that are on their own should be in another place. It's a mixture. All this drama and chaos because they are drinking and taking drugs around you." Having to "climb over crack heads" was also noted. Nodding her head, Taniyah picked up from where Lucy left off: "Yeah, I was right across from a guy. You had to be careful. He was always filthy because he couldn't care for himself, they moved him after because he would come out and pee in the hall. And vomit in the hall. And I had to pass there with my kids every morning to take them out."

Laura (who we first met in Chapter 3) also shared her experiences of her child being groomed in temporary accommodation, yet outrageously, these were safeguarding issues that seemed to be ignored by housing officers. This is not to say that single homeless men aren't themselves vulnerable or in need of shelter, but rather that they should not be placed in the same accommodation as families. There is concern, however, that Labour's decision at the beginning of their tenure in government to release thousands of prisoners early will contribute to already rising homelessness among prison leavers, and that this might lead to increased dangers to the safety of mothers and their children in mixed accommodation.[38] Families are both trapped living in prison-like conditions themselves and risk being forced to co-habit with ex-inmates who have criminal records and mental health conditions, putting homeless mothers and children at further risk.

Stuffed

Families experiencing homelessness and dwelling on the move in England today are not just being endangered by living in temporary accommodation but they are also, in slang terms, "stuffed" (harmed) by the financial and emotional costs of moving and purchasing the stuff of home. Back in 2019, Namono had travelled north by train from London to Manchester. She boarded with her daughter Ruby at Euston Station with just two suitcases and a pram. "I lost most of my things to be honest", she recalled. Namono had been forced to give away or leave everything else because of the costs of relocating and storing her things. The price of life in limbo weighs heavily, literally and metaphorically. Prohibitive moving and storage costs means that repurchasing the basics isn't guaranteed to be a one-off occurrence. For the women we worked with in Greater Manchester, removals typically included taxi rides of around £50 and storage costs often ran into the hundreds of pounds per month. In London, some participants were quoted as much as £500 per month for storage. Makeshift ways of dealing with this peppered our interviews. Irhaa told of her sister enlisting a delivery driver she knew as a favour to move some of her belongings. This proved stressful and was hurried as his van was fitted with a tracker by his employer.

Belle, another of our participants, explained how she started using vacuum storage bags to shrink her worldly belongings and reduce the costs of life on the move. According to online vendors, vacuum storage bags can reduce the size of contents by up to 75 per cent and are "perfect" for making extra space around the home or squeezing more into a suitcase. Belle's shrinking and displacement of her domestic world in an era of austere economics and household debt took us back in time to a project we'd worked on in London five years previously, where our participants had told similar stories.

Stephanie, in the London Borough of Lewisham, was evicted from the private rented sector by her long-term landlord. Borrowing money from her dad had enabled her to keep some of her family's most treasured possessions in a self-storage unit. The storage cost £400 per month and she detailed how insurance costs were additional to this. Moved repeatedly between temporary accommodations, she had asked the local authority, "what about my stuff?" The local authority "didn't want to hear", but then said she could store some of her things in their warehouse.[39] Distrust of the security and cleanliness levels at the warehouse made Stephanie feel "uncomfortable": "you know, it's taken me many years to build up nice things and I'm very OCD and I look after my things". Like the dirtiness she was encountering in temporary accommodation, she did not trust that the council warehouse wasn't also filthy. She explained, "It put me on edge, so I said 'no, I'm not gonna do that'. Also, a friend had loads stolen from her plot in the [council] warehouse and I was like 'oh god'."

Stephanie nonetheless acknowledged what she called her "privilege" to borrow money from a family member. Women with no recourse to any storage are "stuffed" financially and logistically by the number of times they were moved between temporary accommodations. Street Storage, a London-based charity that provides storage of belongings for people who have experienced street homelessness, have pointed out that storage needs in the homelessness sector are consistently overlooked.[40] This is acutely the case for families with children. Added to this, the lack of space in temporary accommodation and the speed at which families are moved between places, with little notice, works against them holding onto their possessions without logistical and financial penalty. The emotional aspects of either having to discard, store or move treasured belongings was captured by artist Simone Brewster at the Homelessness: Framed exhibition at the Saatchi Gallery, London (Figure 5.6).

This mixed-media piece honours a range of different belongings, from mundane necessities of life to those that nourish nutritionally and intellectually, that give comfort and are important to a woman's cultural identity. They are belongings that matter. They are "precious things" that adults and children are stripped of. The description to the side of the installation read:

> Many people staying in temporary accommodation have the possessions from a full and valued life. However these possessions are unable to follow them into their temporary homes and are held in storage,

usually at great personal expense. For some, these possessions are separated from them for months and years, whilst others can no longer afford to keep the storage and lose them forever. It is not only possessions that end up being put on hold, other essential human emotions that have no space for expression must also be put away. This, alongside the lack of a stable and secure home, can lead to lasting trauma, and repeat homelessness.

Figure 5.6 *Pack Away Desire and Other Precious Things*, Simone Brewster, 2024

Source: Photo by K. Brickell, September 2024.

Brewster's description of her artwork captures the acute limbo that Elizabeth, a Black woman in her forties from South London, experienced. Elizabeth was evicted from the flat she rented for six years. The landlord was ready to sell it. When we first met Elizabeth in autumn 2016, she had been given notice on the temporary accommodation flat she'd been placed in.[41] She was about to be moved into PLACE/Ladywell, a purpose-built temporary accommodation development, and had paid a deposit of £50 for a removal van.[42] But a plumbing leak in the award-winning temporary housing scheme put her move on hold. After waiting several weeks, she received a phone call saying, "Okay, Elizabeth, the leakage is fixed. We are only waiting to install the white goods because the property comes with white goods". Elizabeth was just desperate to move in.

> I told her literally, "if by this Thursday the white goods are not ready just let me in. Just let me in. I'll sleep, I'll do launderette outside, buy chicken and chips, but I just can't do the travel, it's just driving me crazy". I'm spending so much on fuel, and the stress ... my daughter is missing out on breakfast because the traffic is just horrendous to get her to school. And I cannot be late for work!

The broken promises of the move date, its shifting and uncertainty, left Elizabeth angry and exhausted. She drove across London to her daughter's school and then the hospital where she worked as a mental health nurse. The costs of the commute were mounting, her daughter often went hungry, she was living among piles of boxes and the additional storage she had rented was adding to her financial stress. She felt literally boxed in. "I've lived my life in boxes, opening them, putting things back in, bringing them out, taping them up, you know?" The removal company had also lost faith and patience, asking, "are you ever going to move into the property?" and threatening her with forfeiting the deposit she'd made. The costs of storing her things also escalated through these delays: "Two weeks turned into a month, then a month turned into another, and then my things were in storage for two months, then after two months because I kept on paying weekly storage, I can't remember how much, it was too much, and I said, 'you know what? Let me move my things into the property'."

In 2024, the UK average storage cost was £27 per square foot with the advice to save money by shopping around and taking advantage of deals typically offered for long-term storage.[43] But how do families find the extra money to move their belongings? How do they have the time to shop around as they are moved from pillar to post? What happens if they are, as happens so often, moved away from the storage facility? And given the unknown wait in temporary accommodation, how can they sign up to multiple-year deals? Life in limbo is financially taxing. It is another form of "poverty tax": hidden costs that people with low incomes face as a result of financial hardship and debt.[44]

The logistics and distances of journeys to employment and school(s) during this limbo also has financial repercussions that work against a family's economic security. Several women, including Christine (whose testimony we heard just before Chapter 3), lost jobs or had to drop down to part-time hours in response to the ever-shifting sands of their housing circumstances. The unknown wait to access permanent housing leaves families unable to plan. When Elizabeth finally moved into PLACE/Ladywell, her stay was anything but temporary. It wasn't until October 2019 that she successfully bid on a permanent tenancy. As another participant in London raged, "I can't plan the next year of my life practically, I can get a phone call and be told everything's gotta be packed up right now, and I haven't got money for a van". This also has financial consequences, "so literally, you've gotta try and keep something back just in case you're told you're moving the next morning . . . it's that quick". Budgeting becomes especially tricky when living with unpredictability as the costs of storage, moves, employment changes and transport all add up. In this sense, debt has an ambivalent character in these moves: it is amassed through the costly and punitive logistics of displacement but also taken on for storage and transportation, as an investment in hope for a future home that will work for their family.

Penalized

Heightened financial pressures in, and moving between, temporary accommodation is aggravated by the costs of what is officially known by the Department for Education as "home-to-school travel". For Casho, who we met in Chapter 3, bus travel was crucial to ensuring her children stayed in their existing schools. She didn't want them to miss out on education and a sense of stability when she moved into temporary accommodation after fleeing domestic abuse. But for each of her children to reach their schools the family was forced to take multiple buses, amounting to 22 single bus journeys, *daily*. The alarm went off at 6 am each weekday morning. Sad-face stickers were pressed by Casho onto the journey map she made with us during our second meeting, depicting the seemingly never-ending cycle of buses that she and her children took each day. Waiting in the rain at bus stops was also something they had come to intensely loathe. That emotion, the excessive time and the financial burdens of travel to and from school had become for them one of many penalties of life in temporary accommodation.

Casho eventually found out that her children were eligible for free school bus passes. But to apply she needed to pay for passport photos, and the wait between applying and receiving the pass could be weeks long. Casho did not have the money for passport photos so had not even been able to apply when we spoke with her. For all the mothers we interviewed, low income levels and debts owed meant that any additional payment – no matter how small – could be the difference between, say, getting the children to school or being able to afford to put the heating on. As Casho put it: "Sometimes food's running out. But the bus, I need to buy a pass again." Until she was able to sort out the free school bus passes, she was having to spend £280 per month on bus journeys: more than a quarter of her total monthly income on home-to-school transport. The Community Impact Lead at a charity aiding homeless families in Greater Manchester attests to how widespread and thorny transport matters are: "it's a case of, do I pay to get the kids to school or do I pay to put the heating on today? It's going to be that level of decision ... there's [often] some small little bureaucratic blockage [that creates further financial problems]."

Costs typically increase as home-to-school distances increase or become more complex with the move into and between temporary accommodation. As per Casho's experiences, however, gaps in eligibility criteria – or the inability to complete applications – mean that people living in temporary accommodation are often unable to access financial support for school bus passes. Nationally, free bus passes are available to both children eligible for free school meals and those whose families are in receipt of the maximum level of Working Tax Credit. But this eligibility tends to extend only to children attending their "nearest qualifying school". At the time of writing, Oldham Council, for example, defines this as the nearest council-maintained school or educational establishment with places available that caters to the age, ability, aptitude and any special educational needs of the child. There are exemptions to this, mainly based on children attending schools further away on religious grounds.[45] These exemptions, however, often do not apply to children who have been placed in temporary accommodation far from their schools. In other words, the "nearest qualifying school" would be a school near to the child's new temporary accommodation. To get the free school bus pass, the child would have to move to that school.

For children experiencing homelessness, school is often the one steady, safe environment in their lives. Moving children to schools local to their current temporary accommodation is extremely risky given they may only be in the area for a short period. Lucy explained, too, that there are also the costs of new uniforms that can push mothers to borrow money: "Once it's paid up, I keep telling myself 'No' [referring to taking out another loan], but like if I'm going to be in a situation then I'm gonna need to. Cause I keep worrying now about school, when they do actually accept them, all new school uniforms."

As Christine told us in her testimony, the costs of school uniform ranges from the uniform itself to all the hidden extras that add up. On top of these hundreds of pounds, all the women we met emphasized the importance of their children remaining in the same school, offering continuity during turbulent times. This included Beatrix who pushed back against the local authority's decision to move her family back to Liverpool. The women we met went to significant logistical lengths to make this happen where possible, walking long distances like Jade (four hours per day) or like Casho changing between, and paying for, multiple buses to get to school. In 2023, Shelter surveyed 1,112 respondents living in temporary accommodation. It found that one in five children had to travel more than an hour to get to school. Temporary accommodation creates havoc in schooling, at times forcing parents to move their children from the schools where they experience safety and familiarity. The same Shelter survey reported that almost half (47 per cent) of families surveyed with school-age children had needed to change their schools because of being moved far from their previous home.[46]

Figure 5.7 Hallway behind the IKEA real roomset

Source: Photo by K. Brickell, March 2023.

No child should be expected to move schools simply because transport is unaffordable. And no local authority in the country should be without transport provisions in place for adults and children living in temporary accommodation. Some local authorities are starting to make this change, including Manchester City Council, whose policy for primary and secondary school children is to support free travel passes for "some children in temporary or homeless families accommodation".[47] Though once under consultation, it is currently not government guidance to include free travel in a local authority's home-to-school travel policy for a child who has been forced to move into temporary accommodation or a refuge.[48] Unless such guidance is made statutory, and the financial means provided to institute it, the country's most vulnerable children will continue to suffer the consequences of the state's failing transport policy.

Life in costly limbo

It was not lost on us that we took the bus to travel home from Hammersmith IKEA. While the mock-up roomset had shown to its customers what the confines of temporary accommodation looks like, life in limbo is more complex than just the four walls they are trapped in. Women's experiences in this chapter reveal the kaleidoscopic variety of negative impacts that a failing state imprints on families. As we set up in earlier chapters, no area of policy failure is left spared. Housing. Education. Social Services. Transport. Discarded, homeless families are being imprisoned in, flung between and hollowed out financially by political choices out of their control.

The mock-up roomset in IKEA was a work of contrast. The temporary accommodation roomset is a shadow of the ideal homes envisaged in the rest of the store. Directly behind it was a hallway roomset, entered through a period-style arch (Figure 5.7). Its interior was adorned with a welcome mat, botanical wallpaper, gentle lavender paintwork, pendant lighting, pale pink flowers, a shoe cupboard and a cushion-scattered bench to ready oneself for the day. All for a room that no one really spends any time in. Unlike temporary accommodation – cramped and overcrowded – where a family's world becomes trapped for weeks, months, even years.

JENNA

"Speaker 1: Lived Experience"
Southampton, 29 November 2023
Women and Homelessness: Research and Practice
Homelessness Community of Practice Network Meeting

To be honest with you it [living in temporary accommodation] was quite traumatizing, especially after coming out of 15 years of abuse with my husband. I had three disabled children. And I was put into a B&B, which was full of men. There was no cooking facilities. There was the tiniest sink, so anything we could wash up, you had to wash up in the shower where we washed. We was all literally in one room.

I had a teenage girl and two young boys, and the boys had got severe autism so that in itself was very traumatizing. I just felt like I was slightly out of area, no support at all, isolated, trying to manage changing over bills and things like that when you've been uprooted. The whole situation was just very overwhelming and just traumatizing in all honesty. And there wasn't suitable accommodation for the children even if they didn't have special needs for such a long period of time. It just made everything a challenge.

I was constantly being retraumatized time and time again. There was no consistency, it was hard to manage routine, with no cooking and washing facilities, having to keep the kids out and active and entertained, then taking them home and trying to do bedtime routine. There's no way for them to play. It affected my mental health and well-being massively and it did traumatize the kids even more so after they'd been through such a traumatic time in their lives. I just felt really alone and really like no one was helping me like and I know obviously I'm really grateful that I managed to get a roof over my head, you know I don't want to say I'm not grateful because I am, it's just it was a very difficult time in my life. . . .

There wasn't much help. I did have this one lady, she worked in temporary accommodation, and she was just one of those people that could relate to you, could connect to you. She just had this way about her that she wasn't patronizing, and she didn't make me keep going over and over things. She didn't just leave me, she made me feel like a human being. She didn't make me feel like I was at the bottom of the pile . . . she even helped me with other things, like it's things like that, that I just look at and I just freak out, and I can't do this because people don't understand when you've been through trauma your brain does not function properly and what you do is you avoid because you can't deal with it because it's it just retraumatizes you every time so then you manage to get yourself in debt or you're not paying your bills and, you know you're even more at risk of street homelessness at that point because you're not meeting your own needs and meeting your life needs basically.

One of the things I hear quite a lot [in my role as a peer mentor] is that women are judged quite a lot. They are constantly being retraumatized. That they just need someone to sit with them, just let them talk, just listen, to help them process their thoughts. Because like I say, you're quite, when you've been in trauma, your thought process is very chaotic and you just need someone to, just say, let's put this in order.

I have an analogy, that there is a big mountain, a cliff if you like [Jenna tips her head upwards as she speaks], and you're looking up the top and you are thinking, I need to get up there and I don't know how. As a peer mentor you say, do you see that little ledge there, how do you think we can get to that bit of the ledge? So, just setting small goals and just *empowering them*, because I must admit, being in that situation, I was just like someone fix me, take all my life, fix it, and let me know when it's done. But the more encouraging thing now I look back is, I was empowered along the way, and actually I know the charity are here, there's a few people that have empowered me massively and other women along the way in different agencies, but it's been really hard work to get the agencies or the services, should I say, *to help*.

I am a fighter, so I'm good at navigating in things like that, and I had a massive support network, but not everyone has that, so just to sit alongside someone and just be there and listen and empathize. A peer mentor is the bridge because we can't all go, have a support worker, have a social worker, because it's tick-box criteria, isn't it? And it's funding, and I know services are stretched, but a peer mentor is that bridge, and to me, people say they feel like a normal person when they're sat with me, "Oh, you understand, or you're not putting pressure on me, you're not making me go over and over things". So, there's definitely great value in what we do.

*

KEYS IN MY HAND,
AND A
NEW PILE
OF SHIT
TO
DEAL
WITH

6

Shit housing: debt beyond homelessness in a failing state

Lucky . . . ?

Knocking on the door of a terraced house on the edge of a Manchester suburb, we were greeted by Alyssa, a participant who you are yet to meet. Her youngest child perched on her hip, Alyssa smiled, invited us in and ushered us to sit down. As we crammed onto the single small sofa in the living room, we were struck by the lack of furniture. The house looked like it had only recently been moved in to, despite the fact that Alyssa and her family had been living there for almost a year. When we asked what the house had been like when she first moved in, Alyssa recalled that it had been totally bare, no furniture, no white goods, not even flooring. Nervous about taking on new debts, Alyssa has been slowly furnishing the house as best she can with her limited funds, prioritizing the flooring and her children's beds. There's no room in her budget for an extra sofa, despite being a household of five – they have to pile on together, or take turns sitting on the floor. Alyssa shrugs: she's been through worse.

Originally from Mozambique, Alyssa and her family moved to Portugal when she was in her early twenties, although her mother and some of her siblings moved to Manchester shortly afterwards in the hopes of finding better work opportunities. After nearly a decade apart, and by this point with two children of her own, Alyssa decided to move to Manchester to be closer to her family. When she first arrived, Alyssa stayed with her mother, but as her younger brother and two of her nieces were already living there, space in the small house was extremely limited. In the hopes of making life more comfortable for everyone, Alyssa and her children moved in with Joseph, a friend of her mothers. Joseph had a one-bedroom flat – Alyssa and the kids slept in the living room. At first things worked out fairly well. Although living conditions were cramped, for £50 a week Joseph had agreed to take her children to school in the mornings, which meant she was able to get a job in a factory and take higher-paying overnight shifts. But this relative stability didn't last. Joseph's already heavy drinking got worse, and he became aggressive, shouting at her and her children for making any noise. Alyssa became concerned for her children's welfare, and felt she had no choice but to leave and declare herself homeless. Her ad hoc childcare situation was also over, meaning that she could no longer take shifts at the factory. Leaving an increasingly dangerous domestic situation had immediately tipped her into further financial precarity.

So began Alyssa's homelessness journey. Initially placed in a hotel room by the local authority, after a few weeks she and her children were moved into temporary accommodation: a small two-bedroom flat. Two years went by, and although the flat was in decent condition, by this time Alyssa was pregnant and increasingly struggling with lugging prams, and her unborn child, up the many stairs. Her imminent new arrival also meant that the already small space was about to become even more cramped. Alyssa prayed that her bids for permanent housing would come to fruition before the baby was born. In summer 2021, her prayers were answered, and she was told her bid on a three-bedroom house had been successful. Alyssa was over the moon and she felt incredibly lucky, particularly as many people she knew were still struggling in temporary accommodation.

As Alyssa regaled us with the story of how lucky she'd been to be offered social housing, we asked her how it felt when she first viewed the property. At this point she laughed, telling us: "I didn't see this house before I bid on it, but when they offered me this house I have to accept." Naively, we were shocked, finding it hard to imagine agreeing to move somewhere, potentially forever, without first being given the opportunity to view it. But this had not been an option for Alyssa. It had been made very clear to her by the local authority that this was essentially her only shot: turn the house down and face being classed "intentionally homeless". Alyssa was nervous about moving to an area she didn't know on the very edge of the city, but she decided to focus on the positives: she and her children were getting a permanent home, a place to feel safe and put down roots. What more could she want?

Unfortunately, Alyssa's happiness and relief was short-lived. Soon after they moved in, her daughter Ella started being severely bullied by the neighbours' children. Racist abuse – shouting slurs at her as she walked by – was soon followed by physical violence. Their young neighbours chased Ella down the street, beating her once they caught up with her. One day, the neighbours attacked Ella again, this time filming themselves kicking her to the ground and posting the video on social media. Ella had been too afraid to tell her mum; the only reason Alyssa found out was because her niece happened to see the video and let her know. Ella now spends most of her time in the house, afraid to go outside and play. Alyssa is terrified to think what might happen next. She's spoken to the police and the local council, but no one seems to be taking things seriously.

Alyssa's story is supposedly one with a happy ending: she is one of the "lucky ones" who lives in social housing. And yet she faces a new trap: one in which she is living in a neighbourhood where her children are in danger, with limited options to leave. She's requested a transfer to another house, but this could easily take years to come to anything because of the dearth of social housing stock and long waiting lists. Or she could leave and attempt to find a house in the private rented sector, opening the family up to the vicious cycle of debt, homelessness and temporary accommodation all over again. Alyssa's story is not unique. It is now common practice for homeless applicants to be given one "suitable" offer of permanent accommodation. If they turn it down, they risk being recategorized as "intentionally homeless", and the local authority are discharged from their statutory responsibilities.[1] This was certainly the experience of many of the women we met. As Lucy, a mother of two young children, recalled: "many, many years ago, when I bid on my flat, I got to go round and see. And then you decide if you like it, want it. Now if you get accepted you cannot even see the property. You have to say yes or no."

For Laura, who we first met in Chapter 3 fleeing from domestic abuse, this lack of choice was even more extreme, as she was pushed to take a house she says she hadn't even bid for:

> I was bidding on houses literally every week, and the house that we got offered they said that I placed a bid on it and I know I didn't. I definitely didn't put a bid on that house, but I got offered it anyway. So I think it was because, they did say . . . they could offer me a house, if one becomes available, and I did have to take it. Because if I didn't I would have been intentionally making us homeless . . . So I love the house. I'm not keen on the area . . . it's rough. I mean I cried when they offered it and then I realized where it was. I went into the housing office to try and fight it, and say I've not put a bid on this property. But you've got to make the best out of a bad situation, I suppose.

For Alyssa and Laura, winning a social housing bid was less a happy ending and more a new series of dangers encircling them as they were forced into taking whatever housing they were offered, regardless of what awaited them when they moved in.

In this chapter we reveal the end of women's homelessness journeys as not an ending at all but rather another point of entanglement in the debt trap. Debt is out-lasting family homelessness, not just triggering and prolonging it. As we explore through the poor standard of housing families are provided with, lack of flooring provision in social tenancies and the ongoing spectre of bill payment, debt stalks families into their new homes.[2] In a failing state, families "move on" from homelessness into a still-shit situation, and shit housing. Will Hutton, current president of the Academy of Social Sciences, wrote in 2018 of "shit-life syndrome", where greater numbers of the populace are struggling to survive and using up all their emotional resources to do so. Problem debt and the unhoming biases of the debt trap tell us so much about the failure to launch what he hoped at the time would be a "multi-pronged assault" on the conditions beyond "shit-life syndrome".[3]

Families' formal homelessness may have ended, but mothers still need to repay existing loans and, at times, deal with the outstanding debts of the former residents of their new homes. Credit, as the sociologist and philosopher Maurizio Lazzarato states, is a "promise to pay a debt, a promise to repay in a more or less distant and unpredictable future".[4] This chapter is testament to the extent of the debt trap's hold on society's most vulnerable, and it again brings to light just how important the little, everyday things are. Without being given the material ingredients of a safe and comfortable home, or the opportunity to earn enough in waged employment to buy them, families in England are being financially floored and are paying the price for a failing state: one that is failing to change course.

Rubbish

Often, what awaits people at the end of their homelessness journey – the supposedly lucky ones for whom there is an end to living in temporary accommodation – is poor quality, badly maintained housing. Research conducted by the Building Research Establishment in 2023 has found that over 200,000 social homes in England have serious hazards, including excessive cold and unsafe stairs. [5] In London, this amounts to one in seven social homes failing to meet the government's Decent Homes Standard.[6] The picture is only getting bleaker – in their 2023–4 Annual Complaints Review, the Housing Ombudsman reported a staggering 329 per cent increase in a single year in interventions to help people in poor quality social housing in England. [7]

Poor quality housing stock, coupled with the erasure of choice in the bidding process, is tantamount to people in temporary accommodation being stripped of their agency. The threat of being declared intentionally homeless renders people largely unable to refuse a house that has been neglected or poorly maintained. This was certainly the case for Taniyah. Like Alyssa, Lucy and Laura, Taniyah, who we first met in Chapter 4, was given no choice on the property she was "offered"; once her bid had been accepted, it was made clear to her that she had to accept or run the risk of being deemed intentionally homeless. Curious, and nervous, she decided to go and take a look at her new home before the move-in date: something that, according to our participants, is generally discouraged by the local authority. As she drove up to the house, her heart began to sink: "When I got here, the yard was full of trash and green nappies and old clothes. And that's not a way to see, well . . . your new house. Yeah, it was horrendous."

She knocked on the door and asked the current tenants if she could take a look inside. Taniyah found the condition of the house to be even worse than the front yard:

> It was dingy and cold. It had no carpets. She … it was nasty, like she used to … just throw everything on the floor. The walls were … She had shit on the walls. Wow, literally poop on the walls. And do you think … they give that to a family?! They [the council] try to clean up as much as they can, but they don't really care. So they gave me a voucher for paint. And I did what I could. I said for Christmas, I'll do it over. But just to get in, I did what I could.

The shit housing literally had shit on its walls. Despite now being privy to the horrendous condition of the house, Taniyah knew she had little choice but to accept the offer and try to make the best of it. This despite knowing that she would immediately be tipped into debt once again in order to make the house liveable for herself and her children. The local authority had given her a voucher for a DIY store, but the condition of the house went far beyond simply needing a lick of paint. As well as being in a generally filthy condition, some of the drains were so severely blocked that raw sewage was leaking into the garden. This meant that the garden was out of bounds for her children, for fear that being out there would make them sick. We visited Taniyah in her new home, and as we stood at the back door, watching a stream of filthy, stinking water flowing past us, she bowed her head, exhausted. Yes, she had a house now, finally. But it was a literal health hazard for her children. Is this what happy endings are supposed to look like?

Laura was also dismayed at the condition of the house she was finally offered after years of living in temporary accommodation: "I shouldn't have done it, but I did. I went round and had a nosey before I actually went for my viewing, but the house was in a real, real bad state. The people that lived there before treated it badly, it was filthy, the garden was piled with rubbish bags." But, like Taniyah, Laura knew there wasn't much she could do about it, even though in her case she was adamant she hadn't even bid for the house in the first place. And, like Taniyah, Laura soon discovered that the condition of the house was even worse than she'd originally thought. In the interim between the former tenants moving out and Laura and her children moving in, the local authority had agreed to let her to do some painting and decorating. It was then that Laura realized the house was infested with bedbugs and rats. This meant that their move-in date was delayed while the infestations were dealt with. Laura and her kids were once again faced with a period of limbo and uncertainty.

Laura's experience is in keeping with national data from the Housing Ombudsman for England reporting that complaints about rat infestations in social housing rose tenfold between 2019 and 2023.[8] Even when permanent housing is provided, its often poor and substandard quality means that debts accrue still further to make the space liveable. Poor insulation, cracks and vermin can often require further borrowing to tackle these issues.

Floored

One of the most common, and costly, contributors to this next layer of the debt trap is flooring. Although homelessness is "over" in the legislative sense, escaping the debt trap can remain difficult and a feeling of being at home hard to find. Lack of provision of flooring or carpets is commonplace in social housing and impacted multiple women who took part in our study, including Evie whose story kicked off the book. Several of the women we worked with told us they took on credit card debt or union credit loans of up to £4,000 to pay for flooring. As Irhaa remarked, "you can't just have your kids on the bare floor". At the time of writing, there are no regulatory requirements in England that floor coverings be provided in social housing lets. Recent research by the Longleigh Foundation has revealed that an estimated 760,000 adults in UK social housing are living without floor coverings, equating to as much as 15 per cent of all social housing households.[9] The financial burden of this for low-income people is huge, and going into debt becomes almost inevitable as families are unable to meet the large up-front costs of flooring. Indeed, the same Longleigh Foundation research estimates that it takes a minimum of 20 months for those on Universal Credit, and eight months for those on low incomes, to repay the cost of floor coverings. This includes not only new builds that are let without flooring but also existing flooring in older properties being removed before the next occupier moves in.[10]

People bidding for social housing are essentially being forced into properties that in many cases are not finished to a liveable standard and are expected to deal with the issues themselves, despite often being in very precarious financial positions. Flooring is an expensive purchase even for those on middling incomes, let alone for people who have so recently been homeless. This new arm of the debt trap was felt acutely by Taniyah. After suffering violence at the hands of her ex, racist abuse from local authority housing officers and appalling conditions in temporary accommodation (covered in Chapters 4 and 5), she had been left to her own devices in a house stripped bare:

> There was no carpet. They ripped everything out. So by the time I paid for the carpet to do the entire house, I was broke. Yeah, I had to borrow from a friend. OK. And when I borrowed from her, she was willing. She gave it to me. She didn't even question. But then, you know, now you have to pay that back. Yeah. So like, every month I pay that.

The horrendous quality of her social housing, and the debt she had been forced into to make it liveable, had completely drained her, emotionally and financially. This was supposed to be a time of relief, their suffering was supposed to be over. As Zofia, who we met in Chapter 3, reflected on hearing Taniyah's story at a group workshop we held: "That's another problem. Yeah, the most the time. Women are very alone and you have the new house and you have to do everything. Everything. The big holes in the wall. Put carpets down. Just how?"

In 2023, largely in response to campaigning from national charities Tai Pawb and Tenant Participation Advisory Service Cymru in Wales, the Welsh government amended its Housing Quality Standard to include the provision of suitable flooring for all social homes.[11] While the rigorousness of its implementation remains to be seen, the amendment highlights that the continuing lack of provision in the English context is indicative of an absence of will. Yet this one small shift in standards would amount to huge relief, both financial and emotional, for a group of people who have already been through unacceptable levels of trauma. To return to one of the prevailing arguments of the book: *the little things matter*. These small acts of neglect can have extremely negative impacts for mothers who are trying to build a home for themselves and their children after periods of horrendous uncertainty and hardship. Yet in England, withstanding a July 2025 proposal to include floor coverings as part of the Decent Homes Standard, the story remains the same for now. Women are left in shit social housing, floored by new debts and asking again, how much debt is a child's tooth worth?

Taxed

In the afterlife of homelessness, debt continues to creep through the cracks. Many of the women we spoke with not only had to face mounting new debts in order to make their social housing liveable, they were also being stalked by past debts, often born of glitches in welfare bureaucracy. For some, new debts were also emerging out of the woodwork of their new homes. The debts of previous tenants. This was most often the case in houses with gas and electricity meters. Low-income single mothers often face the risk of disconnection because of their non-payment in challenging financial times,[12] and they can also find themselves dealing with the outstanding debts from past tenants before access to basic utilities is possible.

After moving delays because of the vermin infestation, Laura thought the house – the one she was given despite never bidding for – was finally ready to move into, only to be faced with yet another barrier when the utility company refused to switch the electricity supply on until the previous tenants' debts had been paid:

> Yeah, I really struggled to get the electric on at the new place ... because there was debt on the meter ... we really struggled, it was a nightmare to get that on. So that prolonged us moving in as well. It does actually affect you. Yeah, like, because they said we won't be switching your supply on until you prove that you're the tenant. So I sent them the tenancy agreement, which was all sent via emails. And they said they wanted a signed copy and I'm like, well, it's all done through emails. It's signed like electronically. How can I do that? So we had to then go and print the tenancy agreement off for me to sign ... A lot of messing about. They wouldn't remove this debt until that was done. Really frustrating. Yeah. So being that close, like, almost got these keys in my hand, and then there's just all this new pile of shit you have to deal with ... other people's debts following you around.

Shit housing and a "new pile of shit you have to deal with" left Laura flummoxed, engaged in a never-ending game of whack-a-mole: "It feels like everything's getting there, and then something else pops up and it knocks you back a bit." How was she ever going to escape the debt trap? Even the house was trapped in debt. Her own problem debt had now collided with someone else's. This spectre of others' debt was also felt by Taniyah, who expressed concern that properties were being "blacklisted" because of previous tenants' debts. Taniyah explained that she had been barred from getting a loan because her address is in debt:

> I know you shouldn't open people's mail, but after a while, I got curious as to why I'm getting rejected [for a loan]. Oh, no, we can't help you. Why? The previous owner is in TONNES of debt. She never paid her light, her water. She never paid anything... but it's so unfair... I've been told, your property is in a lot of debt. I keep on getting sets of bills, you owe this, you owe that.

The struggles described by Laura and Taniyah point to the many layers and complexities of the debt trap. In this case, it is not just people but houses themselves that are indebted. Debt has become so interwoven into England's housing and welfare systems that it has become easy to accrue debts you didn't even know you had: the debts of others, or further debt caused by the bureaucratic complexities of homelessness. Life on the move and regularly changing addresses and tenancy status can lead to confusion relating to bill payments and loss of eligibility for some kinds of income support, including free bus pass eligibility for children. And for some of the women we worked with, changing household circumstances in which either they or their partners found paid employment meant that Universal Credit payments were subsequently deducted, triggering new moments for debt to seep in. For others, debts were being paid off through deductions in the amount of Universal Credit they received each month. This meant that in some instances the women were left out of pocket, with neither their earnings from work, nor their Universal Credit payments, being enough to cover rent, reinstigating the threat of spiralling into debt all over again.

This is all further compounded by insufficient Universal Credit rates that simply do not cover the basics, the minimum five-week wait time for initial Universal Credit payments and the two-child benefit cap, which *still*, as we write, Labour is refusing to fully revoke. This is evidence of a continuing "punitive turn" in welfare, characterized by insufficient financial support and a range of systemic gaps in provision that make indebtedness a near certainty. A joint report by the StepChange Debt Charity and single parents' charity Gingerbread found:

> UC [Universal Credit] is a further driver of income and expenditure shocks. Over half (58%) of single parents affected by the five-week wait had to go without or cut back on food, while over a fifth (21%) said their children had to do the same. 57% indicated that UC had made it harder for them to budget, while just 14% said it had made it easier.[13]

Our interview with a centre manager at a local debt support charity in Greater Manchester revealed the scale of debt accrual because of Universal Credit deductions. She notes that almost none of her clients are in receipt of the full amount of Universal Credit they are entitled to because of various deductions. These are most commonly: deductions for advances given by the Department for Work and Pensions while people are waiting for a Universal Credit claim to start; tax credits (particularly common among mothers whose circumstances are constantly changing, for example when a partner moves back into the home, or having to regularly move home); and utility arrears. These various deductions often create a complex layer of welfare-generated debt that can leave people in thousands of pounds of arrears and consequently with vastly reduced Universal Credit payments.

Citizens Advice have identified Universal Credit deductions as pushing people further into hardship, and clients they help in this situation are typically building up £100 in debt each month, more than double the average for those without a deduction.[14] In the 2024 Autumn Budget, the Labour government lowered the maximum amount a third party can deduct from Universal Credit payments from 25 per cent to 15 per cent. A positive step undoubtedly, but a drop in the ocean in terms of welfare-induced debt accrual.[15] In January 2025, the High Court ruled in favour of a barrister and his client who questioned how deductions by the Department for Work and Pensions to Universal Credit for alleged rent arrears could be legal given the zero consultation or notice given to the tenant.[16] Sudden deductions being made to Universal Credit without any communication of these coming were not uncommon among the women we met. Fear, puzzlement, panic, anger and a lack of control were all reactions that coursed through their bodies and bank accounts.

Alongside the complexities of Universal Credit-related debt, council tax arrears have proved to be a particularly troubling problem.[17] Across England, this is a growing issue, in part because of the classification of council tax arrears as a "priority debt". Figures from Citizens Advice show that their clients who require help for council tax arrears owed an average of £1,370 in 2023, up 21 per cent from 2019.[18] In our conversations with service providers, client confusion regarding council tax payments was cited as a regular means of debt build-up. A debt support team in a Greater Manchester local authority cited council tax arrears as the main criteria for referral to their services, so common is this debt type among financially vulnerable people. The team found that often their clients are not aware when they are eligible for council tax deductions, or that they should be able to arrange personalized repayment plans with the council. This is because support is generally poorly advertised, and people in council tax arrears are instead hit with letters threatening fines and prison sentences if the arrears are not paid off. This dearth of support, particularly for those who are being moved regularly from one temporary accommodation to another, means that the consequences of these debts can escalate quickly. The debt support charity manager we interviewed highlighted that, as well as one of the more complex forms of debt, council tax is also one of the most aggressively pursued. She told us it was not uncommon for clients to be threatened with prison sentences for owing very small amounts. In the case of one of her clients, this amount was as low as £7. This is in keeping with the recent research published by the Money and Mental Health Policy Institute outlined in Chapter 1 that has revealed the scale of brutal council tax debt collection policies across the country.

The prevalence of council tax as a major debt issue was reflected in conversations with our research participants, for whom council tax arrears was a high source of anxiety. Women spoke of bills arriving seemingly out of nowhere, demanding large lump sums they had no idea they owed because of their near-constant moves and changes in circumstance. Jade spoke of the irony of being trapped in a cycle whereby demands to pay off old council tax debts from temporary accommodation she had been placed in years ago meant that she was unable to pay the council tax bill on her current property:

> See, so I don't pay my council tax now because they want me to pay my debt. You want to pay my debt? Plus nearly £200 a month. And I keep claiming for council tax benefit, which I'm entitled to. But they keep sending me back saying that I'm not entitled to it, but when I ring them, they say I am, I apply for it. It takes WEEKS. But then eventually it gets started, you'll only back date for three months. So what about all my other months. They want me to pay my full month plus some on my debt. But I can't afford the £200, never mind my debt as well.

Jade felt completely panicked by the growing pile of bills and had started stacking them up on her staircase, unopened. She told us that she can't bring herself to deal with this new problem: another trauma, stacked up on top of the others. Her journey to this council house had been imbued with trauma – of domestic abuse, of being disbelieved and dismissed by her local authority – she didn't have the emotional capacity to take on new struggles. Jade's experience speaks to the cruel entwinement of mental health issues with debt. To return to the Money and Mental Health Institute's report on government debt collection practices, those with mental health conditions are twice as likely to be behind on council tax repayments as those without them. This is driven by people living with mental health conditions being more likely to have below-average incomes, higher relative costs and difficulties managing money and accessing help.[19] This was certainly reflected in Jade's experience of being trapped in a vicious cycle whereby her previous debts had caused her trauma, and the trauma of those previous debts were contributing to her not being able to face the new debts accrued.

Alyssa felt a similar sense of despair related to her council tax debt. Despite being told she was eligible for council tax support, she had been hit by huge bills that she couldn't pay:

> When I got temporary accommodation, I started to receive big bills for Council Tax. Matt [a charity support worker] would spend hours calling them, to ask them "Why is Alyssa having to pay full council tax?" ... You know, I mean, it was ... £1,000 to pay. In all my life I've never had a problem with bills. And you know, when you receive the bill telling you to pay for something, that you're going to be blacklisted, I don't like this. I have cried a lot about this. They started to send the, you know, the reminder bill in red. You must pay this money by this day. No, I don't have this money. Matt has sent emails to them. He's rung them many times and they say "OK, we'll give this to the manager. We're gonna answer in one week." Every time when we call, we say "Alyssa has Universal Credit, we have sent proof of Universal Credit. We've sent proof of payments. We've sent proof of temporary accommodation, why do you STILL send these bills?

Despite the charity speaking repeatedly with the local authority, and having confirmation that Alyssa was eligible for council tax exemption, she continued to be stalked by council tax debt. This followed her into the supposed safety of her forever home, where once again she was faced with bills for thousands of pounds. Alyssa couldn't cope with the stress of the letters, arriving in increasingly menacing shades of red. The stress had caused her to develop insomnia, lying awake at night, the red letters swirling in her mind. As a result she decided to try and pay off the council tax arrears. In total, she has paid around £1,400 in council tax that she doesn't technically owe. Alyssa's anxiety around council tax was exacerbated by the fact that she is not from the UK and English is not her first language. This made the already complex and opaque welfare system even harder to understand, the threat of prison evoked by council tax arrears letters even more terrifying in the context of a strange and hostile country: "It's very, very, very – I'm scared – because I've never had this [debts] in all my life. And when I have problems and I don't know the solution ... it's hard."

The concept of a poverty tax – that it is more expensive to be poor than rich – is well documented, with indirect taxes – including council tax – being a large contributor to these inequalities.[20] The poorest fifth of people in the UK are spending 28.3 per cent of their disposable income on indirect taxes, compared to just 9 per cent for the richest fifth.[21] For many of the women in our study, council tax is proving to be a huge financial and emotion burden, the continuation of a long line of traumatic events that have pursued them throughout their journey into, and out of, homelessness. These are burdens that have been created by an economic system that breeds inequality. The disproportionate financial weight of poverty has been exacerbated all the more by the cost-of-living crisis that has raged through the UK in the post-pandemic era. The uneven impact of inflation on low-income people is most notable in relation to the rising cost of food, where despite falling inflation towards the end of 2023, the price of budget-range groceries soared by 20 per cent in the same period.[22] Compounded by the value of Universal Credit continuing to fall in real terms, the non-payment of Child Maintenance by ex-partners, the need to service existing loans, the eye-watering costs of childcare and lack of family support to fill these childcare gaps, for society's poorest, debt has become an inevitable necessity to get by in daily life.

Alyssa, like many others, had been pushed time and again into debt. Childcare costs had forced her to resign from the factory post and take lower-paying work with fewer hours. Alyssa's move from temporary accommodation to social housing had also been met with inaccuracies when it came to council tax bills. Financial pressures have been increased further by her now being on maternity leave with her young baby, with even less money to spend on increasingly expensive basics. Sometimes the stress of it all becomes totally overwhelming for Alyssa. She has been let down time and again by a system that has been hollowed out, a system that has lost its humanity: "When you are alone, everything you, you want some days to sit down, cry . . . In this country, it's everything alone."

Happy endings?

As this chapter has shown, even for the mothers who are given their supposedly happy ending of permanent social housing, the debt trap can remain inescapable. Debts accrued through their period of homelessness continue to follow them. Housing stripped bare of floors mean they have little choice but to buy carpets on credit. Red council tax letters appear suddenly demanding huge sums they are unable to pay. And impossibly expensive childcare and an illogical welfare system continue to be a blockade to finding better paid work.

Even for those who find themselves facing racially abusive neighbours, there is nowhere else to go. This is the end point. The options are: return to the private rented sector and face rent arrears and homelessness once again, or finally be offered social housing and be faced with no choice and terrible quality stock. Alyssa's homelessness journey may have ended, but her search for a secure, decent and safe home has not. Instead, her dream of a permanent home has taken on nightmarish qualities. She has been left struggling to find the funds to buy furniture, stalked by council tax debts that turned out to be a local authority error, and fearful of whether the racist abuse towards her daughter from neighbours will escalate. Now, as she struggles to apply for a transfer, Alyssa begins the cycle of waiting and uncertainty all over again: "And now I've made an application, two months ago, they haven't answered me, I don't even have a bidding number."

Despite the hardship she has encountered, a new blockade to finding a home appearing at every stage of her homelessness journey, even at its end Alyssa continues to hope, and fight for, her right to a home. This chapter has revealed how debt continues to pursue and entrap mothers beyond the point of homelessness. And yet, the women we met continue to demand better for themselves and their children: better housing and better treatment from the authorities that are supposed to protect them but more often than not further degrade and humiliate them. As the final chapter attests, the debt trap urgently needs dismantling, in order that exits from homelessness lead to more than the façade of a happy ending. Government needs to be held to account for their contribution to this shit state of affairs. Those in power who reported to Philip Alston, the UN special rapporteur, in 2018 that they were "happy with the ways in which their policies are playing out" need to be held to account.[23] The debt trap is fundamentally the consequence of the devaluation and dehumanization of people – women, people of colour, low-income people – who are deemed unproductive in the neoliberal context. The humanity has been stripped out of policy. This is about more than addressing debt; it is about rethinking what and who society is for.

THERE IS A BIG MOUNTAIN, DO YOU SEE THAT LITTLE LEDGE THERE?

7

Epilogue: dismantling the debt trap

EVIE'S STORY, REIMAGINED

Fizzing sounds of sparklers and starbursts of gold danced out of Evie's phone. These special effects adorned a video of Evie jangling keys outside her new front door, to be sent to friends and family. Her mind wandered back to when she first got the call inviting her to come and view the freshly built social housing. That first visit, the friendly housing officer meeting her at the front door, showing her around her potential new home, asking her whether she was happy with the house. Evie and her three children had been living in temporary accommodation for several months by that point. The accommodation she'd been provided was comfortable enough, and she'd received help and support from her local authority throughout this period of homelessness, but living in uncertainty had been hard on them all.

She put the key into the lock, turned it and stepped into her new home. She smiled. It was as wonderful as she'd remembered. She took off her shoes, enjoying the feel of new carpet under her feet. She took a look around, noting the furniture and white goods that the local council had provided her with. Everything was second hand, a little tired, but it was a great starting point, giving her the breathing room to save for new furniture over time, once she was fully back on her feet. And Evie had been able to bring with her the small numbers of possessions she did have as the costs of moving these had been funded by the local council. The walls were all painted in a colour she loved, one she chose to calm the nervous system with the help of a free, trauma-informed designer for women and children who had experienced domestic abuse.[1] Evie sat down on the sofa, closed her eyes and allowed herself to relax for a moment. Everything was going to be alright. She didn't need to go into debt again to make a home for her children.

Evie's me-time was short-lived, however, disrupted by an alarm that started to chirp in her pocket. How was it school pick-up time already?! The day had gone by in a blur of excitement. She quickly slid her shoes back on and pulled up the hood of her coat. It had started to rain. Thankfully, her children's school was a short walk away. Part of the appeal of this house had been how close it was to their school: somewhere that had remained a constant source of stability throughout this difficult time. Evie remembered the relief she had felt that her local authority had listened to her concerns about being placed in temporary accommodation far from her kids' school. The accommodation they'd been placed in ended up being a 20-minute bus ride away, the closest they'd been able to find in time. But Evie couldn't fault the support she'd received from housing officers, the help applying for free bus passes: something she'd learned all children and their parents/carers staying in temporary accommodation were eligible for. Although this added journey time had been a little tricky, the distance was short enough that it didn't eat into her day too much, enabling Evie to start looking for part-time work.

There was no denying that there had been some severe national economic challenges over the past decade. The 2008 global financial crisis, and the more recent pressures since 2022 on cost of living, largely fuelled by the aftermath of the Covid-19 pandemic and war in Ukraine, had undoubtedly impacted the global economy. But Evie felt grateful that she at least lived in a country whose government seemed invested in supporting society's most vulnerable during these difficult times. Keeping Universal Credit payments, including child benefit, in line with inflation, and prioritizing funding for local authorities, including the building and maintenance of social housing, had kept Evie, and many others like her, sheltered from the worst of the economic hardship. Similarly to the post-Second World War period, working-class and low-income people had been prioritized despite the economic challenges faced.

Evie was aware it hadn't always been this way. Thatcher's Right to Buy scheme in the 1980s had ignited the mass selling of social housing in England, with much of it falling into the credit-fuelled hands of private landlords. Thankfully, successive governments had seen how severely this was diminishing access to affordable housing and decided to scrap it. She'd even heard that at one time there had been talk of rules barring people in rent arrears from bidding for social housing, even if they were homeless, effectively trapping them in temporary accommodation. She shuddered at the thought. She couldn't imagine the horror of becoming homeless because you can't pay your rent, only to find yourself trapped in temporary accommodation because you're in rent arrears, your period of homelessness being extended by the very reason you're homeless in the first place. Evie was thankful that housing ministers had seen and acknowledged how devastating, as well as nonsensical from a financial point of view, such policies would have been. The government had also encouraged more local authorities to exercise preventive measures to help households remain in existing homes by supporting them financially to reduce arrears and avoid eviction. It seemed those in power had the imagination and drive to take on the debt taboo. In response to renter-led protests and acknowledging that before the 1980s private rents were capped and regulated by law, they had also actioned whether and how quickly legal limits could be introduced on how much private landlords could increase rents. Some glimmers of hope, of faith in politicians' willingness to care through material change, were on the country's horizon.

As Evie approached the school gates, she thought about the events that had triggered her brief, but undoubtedly stressful, homelessness journey a few months back. Over the several years they'd been together in private rented accommodation, her ex-partner Lewis had become increasingly controlling, particularly when it came to money. With hindsight, Evie understood that Lewis had used his far higher wage to keep her dependent on him, even for essentials such as food and clothing. When she challenged his behaviour, he retaliated by hitting her. When she called the police, they arrested him and supported her in filing a restraining order against him. But with their tenancy approaching its end and Lewis, the main financial contributor, out of the picture, Evie couldn't keep up with the rent and was issued an eviction notice. Despite recent rises in LHA rates and talks of introducing rent caps in higher-cost neighbourhoods, the private sector remained the least secure form of housing in the country. She'd been very anxious about turning to her local authority for help, but she needn't have been. As soon as she spoke to a housing officer, she felt safe and taken care of, after years of abuse and coercion at the hands of her ex-partner and the more recent stresses of arrears and eviction.

Reflecting on her homelessness journey as she stood at the school gates, waiting to collect her kids, she smiled again. It had been a difficult road for sure. Leaving her abusive partner, the stress of being evicted and living in temporary accommodation had taken its toll. But she'd been supported every step of the way. And now here she was, waiting, finally, to take her kids home.

*

We opened the book with Evie's story. Here, we have reimagined a version of events where Evie, in her darkest hour, encounters systems of governance that support her, that show her compassion and that make her feel valued. Blame and disdain are banished to politics past. Yet our reimagining of Evie's story is far from a utopian one. In this version, she is still abused by her partner, still can't pay the rent in her private sector property, still experiences homelessness. What have been removed are the piecemeal policies, assumptions and behaviours charted throughout this book that set up and maintain the debt trap. In this reimagining, we are advocating for responses to hardship, to indebtedness and homelessness, that are built on principles of dignity rather than shame. We imagine a nation that prioritizes the needs of the most vulnerable, rather than one that reallocates blame for systemic failings to the actions of individual debtors.

Debt Trap Nation urges, in solidarity with other feminist work, a political movement against guilt and the outsourcing of blame to single mothers for personal debts born of factors out of their control. As we posed in Chapter 1, what about the huge debt that society owes women and mothers? This debt is rarely acknowledged, let alone repaid. Yet the debt owed to women and mothers has only intensified under austerity and privatization, as the drive to reduce national debt and increase productivity has effectively failed to deliver on better life experiences, chances and changes for the most vulnerable. How can government say they are "happy" with the impact of their policies (as they did in response to the UN special rapporteur) when shelter, one of the very basics of life, is being denied to hundreds of thousands of children? The moral vacuity of those in power responsible for this dire state of affairs is breathtaking and has resulted, quite literally, in the breath being taken away from babies and children dying in temporary accommodation.

We contend that Evie's reimagined story of hope does not need to remain in the realms of our imagination. A more compassionate and coherent response to poverty, debt and homelessness is possible. Truly listening to women, learning from their experiences, believing them and acting upon their calls for change is essential. Their life stories show how there are no silver bullets here: we are in too deep; the threads of systemic failings that make up the debt trap are too messy, too tangled. But there are instead many opportunities to unpick the mess, piece by piece. As Jenna, the life expert whose story began Chapter 6, so imaginatively suggests, what we need are "ledges" for women and their children to grab on to, as they try and surmount the mountainous task that is dealing with family homelessness, domestic abuse and debt in a failing state.

Some of these "ledges", such as reconsidering punitive housing allocation rules, particularly for domestic abuse victims, or ensuring all people living in temporary accommodation are eligible for free bus travel, could be implemented at speed and would have an immediate transformative effect on families' experiences of homelessness and indebtedness. Others, such as ramping up social housebuilding and investing in the repair and maintenance of existing stock, even if started tomorrow, will take longer for the effects to be felt. But the journey to positive change could begin tomorrow, starting with a renewed political pride in social housing and all it can achieve. "What we haven't heard is how it builds people, how it sets them up for life", Kwajo Tweneboa told hundreds of attendees at Crisis' 2025 Homelessness Summit, in the shadow of Westminster. Likewise, rather than focusing on the "drain" of welfare to the state, what about speaking about the power of benefits in the fight against poverty and as a safety net for those in need?[2] In both instances, the stigma of those living in social housing and/or claiming welfare benefits serves to make indefensible political decisions socially and politically acceptable.[3]

What is essential for truly long-lasting, systemic change is a total overhaul in our understanding of who society is for, who we value within it and how homeless, indebted people are labelled and treated. As the Amnesty International film in Chapter 5 poignantly voiced in respect to homeless mothers and their children: "Until their lives matter to society, they're invisible." Single mothers' contributions to raising children and sustaining communities in the most difficult of circumstances, including being reliant on credit to survive, are being denigrated through modern capitalist logics that exalt only productivity and economic growth and fail to honour and replenish the everyday labours and labourers sustaining life itself. Attitudinal change is the hardest of all to enact, but in the long term this will have the most profound effects. Until these changes – bureaucratic, legal, attitudinal, political – are enacted, the debt trap will continue to traumatize not only the families who are currently homeless and suffering in temporary accommodation but future generations. As the StepChange Debt Charity and the Children's Society noted in a report published over a decade before ours: "another generation of children brought up under the shadow of problem debt is simply not acceptable".[4]

Just as many housing campaigners ask us to imagine living in temporary accommodation to make their case for change, we hope we have helped you to imagine what living within the debt trap is like: being evicted as a result of debt, caught and held in prison-like temporary accommodation by that debt, only to find that life after homelessness doesn't come with an afterlife free from debt. In England today, too many mothers and their children are living out the consequences of limited political imagination.

The subtitles that run through the chapters of *Debt Trap Nation* reflect women's lived experiences of unhomeliness and alienation in a neoliberal nation whose obsession with money and markets has ransacked and harmed the caring infrastructures, human fabric, rhythms and intimacies of everyday life. Controlled, disbelieved, stalked, forced back, abandoned, refused, judged, imprisoned, confined, transient, cleaned out, endangered, stuffed, penalized, floored, taxed. These subtitles capture women's, and especially single mothers', experiences of a nation steeped in violent, misogynist and dehumanizing behaviour. England is caught in a more-than-housing crisis that is failing women, failing families and failing the very youngest in society: children. Now, more than ever, is the time to act, to begin the long and difficult task of dismantling the debt trap.

A note on research methods

Debt Trap Nation is an intervention founded on the life stories of homeless single mothers living in temporary accommodation whom we met through various research projects since 2016, first in London and then later in Greater Manchester. Most of the data presented in the book stem from the later study supported by the Urban Studies Foundation and British Academy. We have worked with past or current clients of the Shared Health Foundation, a charity working to reduce the impact of poverty on health in Greater Manchester. The arguments we make, and views expressed, however, are ours alone.

Between May 2022 and October 2023, we undertook repeat in-depth interviews with 13 women who, along with their children, had been made homeless in Greater Manchester. Eight of the women we worked with were from Black, Asian and minority ethnic communities, and four were migrants (three from non-EU countries). Although coming from a range of different backgrounds, every participant had experience of debt and living in temporary accommodation for three months or more. We met each participant up to three times across a year-and-a-half period. After the first semi-structured interview, we harnessed "journey mapping" in the second session to better understand women's individual housing and financial biographies. This consisted of using key images based on their initial interviews to create a visual map of their journeys into, through and in the aftermath of homelessness, and the varying ways debt accrues and compounds along the way.

The third "exit" interview with each participant focused on updating their journey maps and reflecting on their planned for or imagined futures. Due to concerns for anonymity, we are unable to reproduce the images in the maps because of identifiable information revealed and use pseudonyms instead of participants' real names. We have worked with the illustrator Di Boyle to recreate images and scenes from the journey maps and interviews to represent visually what mothers described.[1] Following the journey mapping phase of the research study, in autumn 2023 we re-met seven of the women to share the overall findings and hear their views and reactions. As part of the research, we additionally interviewed more than 20 key national actors and local frontline staff, councils, support workers and integrated service charities.

In October 2023, we presented a final research report in parliament at a dedicated meeting of the APPG for Households in Temporary Accommodation.[2] In the lead-up to this, we worked with Anthony Luvera, a well-known photographer for capturing the effects of housing inequality, to ensure that the report had visual immediacy and resonance.[3] Since the report's launch, we have submitted evidence to the Women and Equalities Committee's 2023 Inquiry on the "impact of the rising cost of living on women" and the Public Accounts Committee's 2024 "tackling homelessness" inquiry. We have also attended and spoken at different events where women "life experts" have described their encounters with family homelessness and, in several cases, debt. We subsequently undertook several interviews with them and have combined these into our analyses. The many speeches we have heard at these events by political and policy figures have also been folded into our thinking and the writing of this book.

Between January and March 2024, we pushed to understand, at a national level, the impacts that local authorities' respective housing allocation policies are having for indebted homeless families trapped in temporary accommodation. We worked with Fraser Curry at King's College London to investigate housing allocation policies and housing-related debts, which either make an applicant ineligible for social housing or deprioritize their bidding status. We analysed, first, the housing allocation policies of all 294 councils in England (this figure excludes 21 county councils). We found that 99 per cent of policies make reference to "rent arrears" or "debt". In fact, there are over 5,000 mentions of these terms in housing allocation policies nationally. Second, we submitted standardized FOI requests to the 294 councils: 95 per cent of councils replied, albeit many stating that they could not provide any data. Chapter 4 reveals further insights into this new dataset and builds on the media coverage we galvanized in October 2024 on the harmful impacts of these unscrutinized housing allocation rules in England. A second FOI request was sent to all councils; this concerned the provision of cots and safer-sleeping advice in temporary accommodation (these data are found in Chapter 5).

In this book we have harnessed these varying forms of collaboration, methods and strategies to better understand domestic abuse, household debt and family homelessness in a failing state and "speak truth to power". We are strong believers in the importance of research, geographical research in particular, that does not just map injustice but also works in partnership to tackle it.

Notes

1 DEBT TRAP NATION

1. "White goods" are generally domestic large appliances such as fridges, freezers and washing machines.
2. Evie's story is an amalgam of multiple participants' experiences communicated to us in their interviews and showing us the state of their housing when we met in situ.
3. *Statutory Homelessness in England: July to September 2024*, Ministry of Housing, Communities and Local Government, 2024. https://www.gov.uk/government/statistics/statutory-homelessness-in-england-july-to-september-2024/statutory-homelessness-in-england-july-to-september-2024.
4. Emma Bimpson, Sadie Parr & Kesia Reeve, "Governing homeless mothers: the unmaking of home and family", *Housing Studies* 37:2 (2022), 272–91.
5. Julia Krane, *What's Mother Got to Do with It? Protecting Children from Sexual Abuse* (Toronto: University of Toronto Press, 2003).
6. The UK's two-child benefit cap prevents parents from claiming Child Tax Credit or Universal Credit for more than two children. It was introduced by the Conservative government in 2017. In February 2025 it was revealed that the Labour government were considering exempting parents of under-fives from this rule.
7. *Troubled Families Programme: Evaluation Overview Policy Report*, Department for Communities and Local Government, 2017. https://assets.publishing.service.gov.uk/media/5a820863e5274a2e87dc0cb8/Troubled_Families_-_Evaluation_Overview.pdf.
8. *Children Are Living in Families Impacted by the Two-Child Limit Everywhere in the UK*, End Child Poverty, 2024. https://endchildpoverty.org.uk/two_child_limit/#:~:text=The%20annual%20cost%20of%20scrapping,250%2C000%20children%20out%20of%20poverty%20.

9. Kiran Stacey, Aletha Adu & Phillip Inman, "Parents of under-fives may be exempted from UK's two-child benefit limit", *The Guardian*, 26 February 2025. https://www.theguardian.com/society/2025/feb/26/parents-under-fives-could-be-exempted-two-child-benefit-cap-uk#:~:text=As%20well%20as%20exempting%20parents,cost%20of%20£4.5bn.
10. Patrick Butler, Phillip Inman & Jessica Murray, "Record 4.5m children in poverty in UK as cuts condemned as 'morally repugnant' ", *The Guardian*, 27 March 2025. https://www.theguardian.com/society/2025/mar/27/children-poverty-government-benefit-welfare-cuts-uk.
11. Anthony Reuben, "Is there a £22bn 'black hole' in the UK's public finances?", BBC Verify, 3 September 2024. https://www.bbc.co.uk/news/articles/cx2e12j4gz0o.
12. Maudie Johnson-Hunter, Becky Milne, Alfie Stirling & Rachelle Earwaker, "Starmer's missed milestone? The outlook for living standards at the Spring Statement", Joseph Rowntree Foundation, 22 March 2025. https://www.jrf.org.uk/sites/default/files/pdfs/starmer-s-missed-milestone-the-outlook-for-living-standards-at-the-spring-statement-255be15b66c96b828004099abfcff1ce.pdf.
13. "Spring Statement 2025 speech", Gov.UK, 26 March 2025. https://www.gov.uk/government/speeches/spring-statement-2025-speech.
14. "Health and disability benefit reforms – impacts", Department for Work and Pensions, Spring Statement 2025. https://assets.publishing.service.gov.uk/media/67e3fa664038ca2e94411fef/spring-statement-2025-health-and-disability-benefit-reforms-impacts.pdf.
15. James Riding, "Disability benefit cuts will push families into homelessness, charity boss warns", *Inside Housing*, 26 March 2025. https://www.insidehousing.co.uk/news/disability-benefit-cuts-will-push-families-into-homelessness-charity-boss-warns-91149.
16. "Cuts to push 250,000 into poverty as living standards for the poorest under continuing assault", Joseph Rowntree Foundation, 26 March 2025. https://www.jrf.org.uk/news/cuts-to-push-250000-into-poverty-as-living-standards-for-the-poorest-under-continuing-assault.
17. "Personal debt in the UK January–December 2024", in *Statistic Yearbook 2024*, StepChange Debt Charity, 2024. https://www.stepchange.org/Portals/0/23/policy/syb2024/StepChange_Debt_Charity_Research_Statistics_Yearbook_2024.pdf.
18. *Bearing the Burden: Unravelling Women's Debt Dilemma*, Client Insights Report, StepChange, 2023. https://www.stepchange.org/Portals/0/23/policy/burden/Unravelling-Womens-Debt-Dilemma-Report-Nov-23-StepChange.pdf.
19. *What Is Homelessness Like for Women?* Single Homeless Project. https://www.shp.org.uk/homelessness-explained/what-is-homelessness-like-for-women/.
20. *London's Temporary Accommodation Emergency*, Housing Committee, London Assembly, 2024. https://www.london.gov.uk/sites/default/files/2024-03/

Housing%20Committee%20-%20Temporary%20Accommodation%20 report.pdf.

21. *Single Parents in 2023*, Gingerbread. https://www.gingerbread.org.uk/our-work/policy-and-campaigns/research-publications/single-parents-in-2023/.
22. "Domestic abuse victim characteristics, England and Wales: year ending March 2024", Office for National Statistics, 2024. https://www.ons.gov.uk/peoplepopulationandcommunity/crimeandjustice/bulletins/domesticabuseinenglandandwalesoverview/november2024.
23. "Domestic abuse victim characteristics, England and Wales: year ending March 2023", Office for National Statistics, 2023. https://www.ons.gov.uk/peoplepopulationandcommunity/crimeandjustice/articles/domesticabusevictimcharacteristicsenglandandwales/yearendingmarch2023.
24. "Domestic abuse prevalence and trends, England and Wales: year ending March 2024", Office for National Statistics, 2024. https://www.ons.gov.uk/peoplepopulationandcommunity/crimeandjustice/bulletins/domesticabuseinenglandandwalesoverview/november2024.
25. "Statutory homelessness in England: July to September 2024", Ministry of Housing, Communities and Local Government. https://www.gov.uk/government/statistics/statutory-homelessness-in-england-july-to-september-2024/statutory-homelessness-in-england-july-to-september-2024.
26. Dana Abed & Fatima Kelleher, "The assault of austerity: how prevailing economic policy choices are a form of gender-based violence", Oxfam, 2022. https://www.oxfamnovib.nl/Redactie/Downloads/Rapporten/The%20Assault%20of%20Austerity_final%20briefing%20paper.pdf.
27. "Witness statement of Helen MacNamara", UK Covid-19 Inquiry, 9 October 2023. https://COVID-19.public-inquiry.uk/wp-content/uploads/2023/11/03103311/INQ000273841.pdf.
28. Address by President Nelson Mandela at the launch of the Nelson Mandela Children's Fund, Pretoria, 8 May 1995. http://www.mandela.gov.za/mandela_speeches/1995/950508_nmcf.htm.
29. "112,000 and counting", Justlife, 1 May 2024. https://www.justlife.org.uk/news/2024/how-to-reduce-numbers-in-homeless-temporary-accommodation.
30. Hansard HC Deb. Vol. 752 (debated on Tuesday 30 July 2024). https://hansard.parliament.uk/commons/2024–2007–30/debates/1f2d41ab-d38d-4f29-b6c7–1e67179c2bf5/CommonsChamber.
31. "Council tax: non-payment", UK Parliament, 2025. https://questions-statements.parliament.uk/written-questions/detail/2025-01-13/23550.
32. Toby Murray & Francesca Smith, "In the public interest? The psychological toll of local and national government debt collection practices", Money and Mental Health Policy Institute. https://www.moneyandmentalhealth.org/publications/in-the-public-interest/.
33. Patrick Butler and Josh Halliday, "Ministers urged to act as thousands more hit by UK carer's allowance debts", *The Guardian*, 21 March 2025. https://

www.theguardian.com/society/2025/mar/21/ministers-urged-to-act-as-thousands-more-hit-by-uk-carers-allowance-debts.

34. Josh Halliday, "Mother of autistic boy left with £10,000 debt after breaching DWP rules by £1.92 a week", *The Guardian*, 3 May 2025. https://www.theguardian.com/society/2025/may/03/mother-of-autistic-boy-left-with-10000-debt-after-breaching-dwp-rules-by-192-a-week.
35. Richard Partington, "Almost half of England's councils 'could face bankruptcy over £4.6bn deficit'", *The Guardian*, 28 February 2025. https://www.theguardian.com/society/2025/feb/28/almost-half-of-englands-councils-could-face-bankruptcy-over-deficit.
36. "Local Authority finance: a decade of debt", National Institute of Economic and Social Research, 2024. https://www.niesr.ac.uk/publications/local-authority-finance?type=general-election-briefing.
37. Kwajo Tweneboa, *Our Country in Crisis: Britain's Housing Emergency and How We Rebuild* (London: Trapeze, 2024), 68.
38. "Women in work 2024", PwC. https://www.pwc.co.uk/services/economics/insights/women-in-work-index.html.
39. "Keir Starmer speech at Labour Party Conference 2024", Labour.org.uk. https://labour.org.uk/updates/press-releases/keir-starmer-speech-at-labour-party-conference-2024/.
40. Danny Dorling, *Shattered Nation: Inequality and the Geography of a Failing State* (London: Verso, 2023).
41. David Graeber, *Debt: The First 5000 Years* (London: Melville House, 2012), 379, emphasis in original.
42. David Bond & Claire Donovan, "The extent of furniture poverty in the UK", End Furniture Poverty, 2023. https://endfurniturepoverty.org/wp-content/uploads/2023/05/The-Extent-of-Furniture-Poverty-in-the-UK-final-3.pdf.
43. Sorcha Mahony & Larissa Pople, *Life in the Debt Trap: Stories of Children and Families Struggling with Debt* (Bristol: Bristol Policy Press, 2018), 85.
44. "Pull your socks up" is a British idiom that means to try to improve your behaviour or work, especially if it's not good enough.
45. Christine and Jenna have given us permission to print their "life expert" talks in our book. Sam's story is part of an IKEA/Shelter collaboration and is available publicly online and was displayed at the IKEA store we visited.
46. All names of participants in the book are changed to pseudonyms, except where they requested and consented to their real first name being used. Participants were given upwards of £25/session in Love2Shop vouchers to reflect the time and expertise they shared with us.

2 NOT AT HOME IN A FAILING STATE

1. "The right to adequate housing", Fact Sheet 21, UN Habitat, 2014. https://www.ohchr.org/sites/default/files/Documents/Publications/FS21_rev_1_Housing_en.pdf.

2. *The Debt Trap: Exposing the Impact of Problem Debt on Children*, StepChange Debt Charity and The Children's Society, 2014, 2.
3. "The UK's household debt crisis", Debt Justice, 2023, 2. https://debtjustice.org.uk/wp-content/uploads/2022/09/Household-Debt-Briefing.pdf.
4. *In Work: But Still in Debt*, StepChange, Client Insights Report, April 2024. https://www.stepchange.org/Portals/0/23/policy/in-work-still-in-debt/in-work-still-in-debt-stepchange-april-2024-web.pdf.
5. "Financial Lives cost of living (Jan 2024) recontact survey – summary", Financial Conduct Authority. https://www.fca.org.uk/publications/financial-lives/jan-2024-recontact-survey-summary.
6. Benedict Guindi & Tilly Cook, *Unavoidable Debt*, Citizens Advice, 2021. https://www.citizensadvice.org.uk/Global/CitizensAdvice/Debt%20and%20Money%20Publications/Unavoidable%20debt.pdf.
7. Susanne Soederberg, *Debtfare States and the Poverty Industry: Money, Discipline, and the Surplus Population* (New York: Routledge, 2014).
8. "Financial Lives 2022 survey: insights on vulnerability and financial resilience relevant to the rising cost of living", Financial Conduct Authority, 2022. https://www.fca.org.uk/data/financial-lives-2022-early-survey-insights-vulnerability-financial-resilience.
9. Mia Gray, "Debt begets debt: public and private debt in austerity Britain", in Jodi Gardner, Mia Gray & Katharina Moser (eds), *Debt and Austerity* (Cheltenham: Elgar, 2020).
10. "Universal Credit statistics, 29 April 2013–11 January 2024", Department for Work and Pensions. https://www.gov.uk/government/statistics/universal-credit-statistics-29-april-2013-to-11-january-2024/universal-credit-statistics-29-april-2013-to-11-january-2024.
11. Sarah Butler, "Cost of supermarket budget brands rose 20.3% in year to December, survey finds", *The Guardian*, 18 January 2023. https://www.theguardian.com/business/2023/jan/18/cost-of-supermarket-budget-brands-rose-203-in-december-survey-finds.
12. Michael Race, "Inflation jumps on food, air fares and school fees", BBC News, 19 February 2025. https://www.bbc.co.uk/news/articles/c0l18pzrz00o.
13. Paul Bolton & Iona Stewart, "Research briefing: domestic energy prices", House of Commons Library, 10 December 2024. https://commonslibrary.parliament.uk/research-briefings/cbp-9491/.
14. "Living on empty: a policy report from Citizens Advice", Citizens Advice, 2023. https://wearecitizensadvice.org.uk/living-on-empty-245f4b9acbe3#8556.
15. "Impact of increased cost of living on adults across Great Britain: September 2022 to January 2023", Office for National Statistics. https://www.ons.gov.uk/peoplepopulationandcommunity/personalandhouseholdfinances/expenditure/articles/impactofincreasedcostoflivingonadultsacrossgreatbritain/september2022tojanuary2023.
16. "One in four people unlikely to talk about debt problems to a loved one",

StepChange Debt Charity, 24 March 2025. https://www.stepchange.org/media-centre/press-releases/one-in-four-unlikely-to-talk-about-debt.aspx.

17. Imogen Tyler, *Stigma: The Machinery of Inequality* (London: Bloomsbury, 2020), 169.
18. Philip Alston, "Press conference of the UN special rapporteur, 2018", YouTube. https://www.youtube.com/watch?v=NeozhyFY1i8.
19. *Ibid.*
20. Philip Alston, "I proved that austerity destroys lives and all the government has done is try to discredit me", *The Independent*, 27 June 2019. https://www.independent.co.uk/voices/austerity-tory-government-theresa-may-philip-alston-un-rapporteur-a8977251.html.
21. Kevin Farnsworth & Zoe Irving, "Austerity: neoliberal dreams come true?", *Critical Social Policy* 38:3 (2018), 461.
22. Tola Onanuga, "Emergency budget: George Osborne's speech in full", *The Guardian*, 22 June 2010. https://www.theguardian.com/uk/2010/jun/22/emergency-budget-full-speech-text.
23. Hansard HC Deb. Vol. 755, "Fiscal rules" (debated on Monday 28 October 2024). https://hansard.parliament.uk/commons/2024-10-28/debates/A486A5B2-6992-46A0-A4C9-0357569BD9DD/FiscalRules#main-content.
24. Stephanie Kelton, *The Deficit Myth: Modern Monetary Theory and How to Build a Better Economy* (London: John Murray, 2020), 19.
25. *Ibid.*, 20.
26. "*The Guardian* view on Labour's welfare plans: betraying the vulnerable", *The Guardian* editorial, 12 March 2025. https://www.theguardian.com/commentisfree/2025/mar/12/the-guardian-view-on-labours-welfare-plans-betraying-the-vulnerable.
27. Johanna Montgomerie, "Austerity and the household: the politics of economic storytelling", *British Politics* 11 (2016), 464.
28. Toby Helm & Daniel Boffey, "Ministers admit family debt burden is set to soar", *The Guardian*, 2 April 2011. https://www.theguardian.com/politics/2011/apr/02/family-debt-burden-government-figures.
29. Mia Gray, Katharina Möser & Jodi Gardner, "Understanding low-income debt in a high-income country", in Gardner, Gray & Möser, *Debt and Austerity*, 2.
30. Paul Krugman, "Austerity games, here and there", *New York Times*, 30 March 2011. https://archive.nytimes.com/krugman.blogs.nytimes.com/2011/03/30/austerity-games-here-and-there/.
31. Jamie Peck, "Austerity urbanism: American cities under extreme economy", *City* 16:6 (2012), 647.
32. Hulya Dagdeviren, Jiayi Balasuriya, Sheila Luz, Ali Malik & Haider Shah, "Financialisation, welfare retrenchment and subsistence debt in Britain", *New Political Economy* 25:2 (2020), 160.
33. "Statutory homelessness in England: July to September 2024", Ministry of Housing, Communities and Local Government. https://www.gov.uk/government/statistics/statutory-homelessness-in-england-july-to-

september-2024/statutory-homelessness-in-england-july-to-september-2024.
34. "Statutory homelessness in England: January to March 2024", Ministry of Housing, Communities, and Local Government. https://www.gov.uk/government/statistics/statutory-homelessness-in-england-january-to-march-2024/statutory-homelessness-in-england-january-to-march-2024.
35. "Statutory homelessness in England: financial year 2023–24", Ministry of Housing, Communities and Local Government, 3 October 2024. https://www.gov.uk/government/statistics/statutory-homelessness-in-england-financial-year-2023-24/statutory-homelessness-in-england-financial-year-2023-24#temporary-accommodation.
36. "Statutory homelessness in England: 2022–23", Department for Levelling Up, Housing and Communities.
37. "No child should be homeless: how housing instability affects a child's GCSE grades", Children's Commissioner, 28 March 2025. https://www.childrenscommissioner.gov.uk/blog/no-child-should-be-homeless-how-housing-instability-affects-a-childs-gcse-grades/.
38. Sammy Gecsoyler, "London councils buy £140m of property to move homeless people out of city", *The Guardian*, 8 March 2025. https://www.theguardian.com/society/2025/mar/08/london-councils-buy-140m-property-move-homeless-people-out-city.
39. Claire Hamilton, "London council to buy Liverpool City Region houses", BBC News, 12 March 2025. https://www.bbc.co.uk/news/articles/cge1zyz7ljwo.
40. "Statutory homelessness in England: January to March 2024", Ministry of Housing, Communities, and Local Government.
41. Wendy Wilson and Cassie Barton, "Tackling the under-supply of housing in England", House of Commons Library, 19 May 2023. https://researchbriefings.files.parliament.uk/documents/CBP-7671/CBP-7671.pdf.
42. "Levelling Up and Regeneration Bill: second reading briefing", Shelter, 2022. https://england.shelter.org.uk/professional_resources/policy_and_research/policy_library/levelling_up_and_regeneration_bill_second_reading.
43. "Loss of social housing", Shelter. https://england.shelter.org.uk/support_us/campaigns/social_housing/loss_of_social_housing.
44. "Renting from a private landlord", Gov.UK, 8 August 2023. https://www.ethnicity-facts-figures.service.gov.uk/housing/owning-and-renting/renting-from-a-private-landlord/latest/.
45. Vicky Spratt, *Tenants: The People on the Frontline of Britain's Housing Emergency* (London: Profile, 2022).
46. "Financial Lives 2022 survey", Financial Conduct Authority.
47. Spratt, *Tenants*.
48. "Number of households facing eviction in private rented sector at highest point in eight years", Crisis, 2023. https://www.crisis.org.uk/about-us/crisis-media-centre/number-of-households-facing-eviction-in-private-rented-sector-at-highest-point-in-eight-years/.

49. Glen Bramley, Suzanne Fitzpatrick, Jill McIntyre & Sarah Johnsen, "Homelessness amongst Black and minoritised ethnic communities in the UK: a statistical report on the state of the nation", Institute for Social Policy, Housing and Equalities Research, Heriot Watt University, 2022. https://researchportal.hw.ac.uk/en/publications/homelessness-amongst-black-and-minoritised-ethnic-communities-in-.
50. "Homes sold under Right to Buy now owned by private landlords", New Economics Foundation, 2024. https://neweconomics.org/2024/05/more-than-4-in-10-council-homes-sold-under-right-to-buy-now-owned-by-private-landlords.
51. *Ibid.*
52. "English Housing Survey 2021 to 2022: private rented sector", Ministry of Housing, Communities, and Local Government. https://www.gov.uk/government/statistics/english-housing-survey-2021-to-2022-private-rented-sector/english-housing-survey-2021-to-2022-private-rented-sector.
53. "English Private Landlord Survey 2021: main report", Department for Levelling Up, Housing and Communities. https://www.gov.uk/government/statistics/english-private-landlord-survey-2021-main-report/english-private-landlord-survey-2021-main-report--2.
54. Dinyar Godrej, "How private equity eroded the right to housing", *New Internationalist*, 9 August 2019. https://newint.org/features/2019/06/19/unitednations-leilanifarha-housing.
55. "Private equity sets its sights on UK's housing market", *City Wire*, 13 June 2024. https://citywire.com/new-model-adviser/news/private-equity-sets-its-sights-on-uk-s-housing-market/a2443966.
56. Gemma Sherlock, "Andy Burnham wants to suspend Right to Buy scheme", BBC News, 7 May 2024. https://www.bbc.co.uk/news/articles/c88z93vm0y5o.
57. Claer Barrett, "Debt is one of the last taboos". LinkedIn post, 2025. https://www.linkedin.com/posts/claer-barrett-74088414_debtfree-debtfree community-activity-7303008042902601729-HdwR.
58. James D. G. Wood, "The integrating role of private homeownership and mortgage credit in British neoliberalism", *Housing Studies* 33:7 (2018), 993–1013.
59. Aiden Greenall, "Debt time bomb: countdown to a household debt disaster", Citizens Advice, 14 July 2023. https://wearecitizensadvice.org.uk/debt-time-bomb-countdown-to-a-household-debt-disaster-e596d10996fe.
60. Nick Bano, *Against Landlords: How to Solve the Housing Crisis* (New York: Verso, 2024), 4–5, 15.
61. Graeber, *Debt*, 48.
62. Tyler, *Stigma*, 18.
63. Graeber, *Debt*, 5.
64. Carl Walker, "Personal debt, cognitive delinquency and techniques of

governmentality: neoliberal constructions of financial inadequacy in the UK", *Journal of Community and Applied Social Psychology* 22:6 (2012), 533.

65. Lucí Cavallero and Verónica Gago, *A Feminist Reading of Debt* (London: Pluto, 2021), 4.
66. *Ibid.*, 3, emphasis in original.
67. *Ibid.*, 4.
68. Silvia Federici, "From commoning to debt: financialization, micro-credit and the changing architecture of capital accumulation", CADTM, 14 June 2016, 183. https://www.cadtm.org/From-Commoning-to-Debt.
69. Nancy Fraser, *Cannibal Capitalism: How our System Is Devouring Democracy, Care, and the Planet – and What We Can Do about It* (New York: Verso, 2022), 49.
70. Federici, "From commoning to debt".
71. Claire Lally, "Consumer debt and mental health", UK Parliament POSTnote 732, 21 October 2024. https://researchbriefings.files.parliament.uk/documents/POST-PN-0732/POST-PN-0732.pdf.
72. Ryan Davey, "Debt", in The Open Encyclopedia of Anthropology, 25 March 2024. http://doi.org/10.29164/24debt.
73. Nicola Henry & Anastasia Powell, "Embodied harms: gender, shame, and technology-facilitated sexual violence", *Violence Against Women* 21:6 (2015), 758–79.
74. "Home: the intimacy of debt and inequality", Data Thistle. https://www.datathistle.com/event/2066389-home-the-intimacy-of-debt-and-inequality/.
75. For more on the research study, see "Festival show will see academic's research project on the big stage", King's College London, 28 February 2023, https://www.kcl.ac.uk/news/festival-show-will-see-academics-research-project-on-the-big-stage; there are also two podcasts via https://www.amazon.in/Housing-Debt-Flying-High/dp/B0C624G4XM.
76. Gustav Peebles, "The anthropology of credit and debt", *Annual Review of Anthropology* 39:1 (2010), 225–40.
77. Susan K. Sell & Owain Williams, "Health under capitalism: a global political economy of structural pathogenesis", *Review of International Political Economy* 27:1 (2010), 1–25.
78. For example, Jayne Haynes, "'Like a prison': the tower block for homeless families that has 8pm curfew and no visitors allowed", *Birmingham Mail*, 3 August 2024. https://www.birminghammail.co.uk/news/midlands-news/like-prison-tower-block-homeless-29645171.
79. Laura Goldsack, "A haven in a heartless world? Women and domestic violence". In Tony Chapman and Jenny Hockey (eds), *Ideal Homes?* (London: Routledge, 1999).
80. Evan Stark, *Coercive Control: How Men Entrap Women in Personal Life* (Oxford: Oxford University Press, 2007).
81. Rachel Pain, "Collective trauma? Isolating and commoning gender-based violence", *Gender, Place and Culture* 29:12 (2022), 1788–809.

82. "Nearly one million UK women trapped with a dangerous abuser because of economic abuse", Surviving Economic Abuse, 26 November 2024. https://survivingeconomicabuse.org/news/one-million-women-trapped/.
83. Joe Richardson & Adam Butler, *The Single Parent Debt Trap*, StepChange and Gingerbread, 2021. https://www.stepchange.org/policy-and-research/single-parent-debt-trap.aspx.
84. Barry Schwartz, "Waiting, exchange, and power: the distribution of time in social systems", *American Journal of Sociology* 79:4 (1974), 856.
85. "Statutory homelessness in England: 2022–23", Department for Levelling Up, Housing and Communities.
86. Deirdre Conlon, "The spectacle of invisibility: vanishing points and the spatialised legal violence of the UK's expanding quasi-carceral geography of immigration control", *Geopolitics*, October (2024): 1–32.
87. Alexander Wakelam, *Credit and Debt in Eighteenth-Century England: An Economic History of Debtors' Prisons* (Abingdon: Routledge, 2020).
88. Margot Finn, "Being in debt in Dickens' London: fact, fictional representation and the nineteenth-century prison", *Journal of Victorian Culture* 1:2 (1996), 203.
89. Ruth Wilson-Gilmore, *Abolition Geography: Essays towards Liberation* (London: Verso, 2023), 747.
90. "London boroughs look to budget for renewed support amid £700m shortfall", London Councils (2024). https://www.londoncouncils.gov.uk/news-and-press-releases/2024/london-boroughs-look-budget-renewed-support-amid-ps700m-shortfall.
91. Stephan Delahunty, Peter Apps & Vicky Spratt, "Inside the economics of temporary accommodation", *Inside Housing*, 22 February 2025. https://www.insidehousing.co.uk/insight/inside-the-economics-of-temporary-accommodation-90656.
92. Deborah Garvie, "Cashing in: how a shortage of social housing is fuelling a multimillion-pound temporary accommodation sector", Shelter, February 2020. https://england.shelter.org.uk/professional_resources/policy_and_research/policy_library/briefing_cashing_in_-_how_a_shortage_of_social_housing_is_fuelling_a_multimillion-pound_temporary_accommodation_sector.
93. Darren Baxter & Joseph Elliot, "Bringing private homes into social ownership can rewire the housing system", Joseph Rowntree Foundation, 31–2. https://www.jrf.org.uk/sites/default/files/pdfs/bringing-private-homes-into-social-ownership-can-rewire-the-housing-system-03d0a6794bc2d28402823ea5078d4da5.pdf.
94. "Children in temporary accommodation: oral evidence", Housing, Communities and Local Government Committee, 5 November 2024. https://committees.parliament.uk/event/22194/formal-meeting-oral-evidence-session/.
95. Naomi Klein, "Disaster capitalism", *Harper's Magazine* 315 (2007), 47–58.

96. Grace Blakeley, *Vulture Capitalism: Corporate Crimes, Backdoor Bailouts, and the Death of Freedom* (New York: Simon & Schuster, 2024).
97. Chris Foye & Edward Shephard, "How big UK housebuilders have remained profitable without meeting housing supply targets", *The Conversation*, 28 November 2023. https://theconversation.com/how-big-uk-housebuilders-have-remained-profitable-without-meeting-housing-supply-targets-215757.
98. Liam Geraghty, "Council spending on homelessness triples in eight years", *Big Issue*, 2 July 2024. https://www.bigissue.com/news/housing/councils-spending-homelessness-temporary-accommodation/.
99. "Local Government Association Conference: a speech from the deputy prime minister", Gov.UK, 24 October 2024. https://www.gov.uk/government/speeches/local-government-association-conference.
100. "Local Government White Paper", Local Government Association, 7 June 2024. https://www.local.gov.uk/publications/local-government-white-paper.
101. "Robbing Peter to pay Paul" is a phrase from English folklore. It refers to taking from one person to give to another: to repay one debt by taking on another.
102. An "Individual Voluntary Arrangement" is a formal and legally binding agreement with an individual and their creditors to pay back debts over a period of time.

3 INDEBTED (AFTER) LIVES OF DOMESTIC ABUSE

1. "Gaslighting" is defined by the National Domestic Violence Hotline website as "an extremely effective form of emotional abuse that causes a victim to question their own feelings, instincts, and sanity". It is bound up with power dynamics: "once an abusive partner has broken down the victim's ability to trust their own perceptions, the victim is more likely to stay in the abusive relationship".
2. According to the UK's Domestic Abuse Act 2021, behaviour is "abusive" if it consists of any of the following: (1) physical or sexual abuse; (2) violent or threatening behaviour; (3) controlling or coercive behaviour; (4) economic abuse; or (5) psychological, emotional or other abuse. It does not matter whether the behaviour consists of a single incident or a course of conduct. The Domestic Abuse Act 2021 legislates that economic abuse is any behaviour that has a substantial adverse effect on a person's ability to "(a) acquire, use or maintain money or other property, or (b) obtain goods or services". See https://www.legislation.gov.uk/ukpga/2021/17/section/1/enacted.
3. "What is economic abuse?", Surviving Economic Abuse. https://survivingeconomicabuse.org/what-is-economic-abuse/.
4. Savannah Dawsey-Hewitt, Tanisha Jnagel, Sangeeta Kalia, Kathryn Royal, Sarika Seshadri, Lindsay Sutherland, Jasna Magić, Madeleine McGivern & Rosa Wilson Garwood, "Shadow pandemic: shining a light on domestic abuse during Covid", Women's Aid, 2021. https://www.womensaid.org.uk/wp-content/uploads/2021/11/Shadow_Pandemic_Report_FINAL.pdf.

5. Ria Ivandić, Tom Kirchmaier & Ben Linton, "Changing patterns of domestic abuse during Covid-19 lockdown", Centre for Economic Performance, November 2020. https://cep.lse.ac.uk/pubs/download/dp1729.pdf.
6. Women's Aid, *The Domestic Abuse Report 2022*. https://www.womensaid.org.uk/wp-content/uploads/2022/03/The-Domestic-Abuse-Report-2022-The-Annual-Audit.pdf.
7. Abed & Kelleher, *The Assault of Austerity*.
8. Jane Krishnadas & Sophia Taha, "Domestic violence through the window of the COVID-19 lockdown: a public crisis embodied/exposed in the private/domestic sphere", *Journal of Global Faultlines* 7:1 (2020), 47.
9. Dawsey-Hewitt *et al.*, "Shadow pandemic".
10. "Domestic abuse victims died as too few women decision-makers, Covid inquiry hears", ITV News, 1 November 2023. https://www.itv.com/news/2023-11-01/uk-was-on-back-foot-early-in-pandemic-due-to-brexit-key-ex-aide-says.
11. "Oral evidence: work of the victims' commissioner", HC 305, House of Commons, 28 April 2020. https://committees.parliament.uk/oralevidence/319/html/.
12. In temporary accommodation, as standard, council tax and other bills such as gas, electricity and water are required to be paid.
13. Sarah Davidge & Lizzie Magnusson, *The Domestic Abuse Report 2019: The Economics of Abuse*, Women's Aid, 7. https://www.womensaid.org.uk/wp-content/uploads/2019/03/Economics-of-Abuse-Report-Summary-2019.pdf.
14. "The cost of Covid-19: economic abuse throughout the pandemic", Surviving Economic Abuse, 2021. https://survivingeconomicabuse.org/wp-content/uploads/2021/04/SEA-Cost-of-Covid-Report_2021-04.pdf.
15. Yvonne Roberts, "'He took every penny': the women left with a debt mountain by coercive partners", *The Guardian*, 3 September 2023. https://www.theguardian.com/society/2023/sep/03/he-took-every-penny-the-women-left-with-a-debt-mountain-by-coercive-partners.
16. Greater Manchester Domestic Abuse Helpline. https://www.domesticabusehelpline.co.uk/our-services/greater-manchester-domestic-abuse-helpline/.
17. "What is economic abuse?", Surviving Economic Abuse.
18. Section 115 of the Immigration and Asylum Act 1999 states that a person will have "no recourse to public funds" if they are "subject to immigration control". This means they have no entitlement to the majority of welfare benefits, including income support, housing benefit and a range of allowances and tax credits. See https://www.londoncouncils.gov.uk/our-key-themes/asylum-migration-and-refugees/no-recourse-public-funds.
19. "Safety before status: how to ensure the victims and prisoners bill meets the needs of all victims", The Domestic Abuse Commissioner for England and Wales, briefing, 2022. https://domesticabusecommissioner.uk/wp-content/uploads/2022/12/Safety-before-status-The-Solutions.pdf.
20. Rosa dos Ventos Lopes Heimer, "Bodies as territories of exception: the

coloniality and gendered necropolitics of state and intimate border violence against migrant women in England", *Ethnic and Racial Studies* 46:7 (2023), 1379.

21. Halliki Voolma, "'I must be silent because of residency': barriers to escaping domestic violence in the context of insecure immigration status in England and Sweden", *Violence Against Women* 24:15 (2018), 1840.
22. Bec Woolley, "Supporting victims of sexual and gender based violence who have no recourse to public funds", Public Health Wales NHS Trust, 2023. https://acehubwales.com/wp-content/uploads/2023/07/PHW-NRPF-report-Eng-5.pdf.
23. "Half of teachers in England work with homeless children", Shelter, 22 December 2023. https://england.shelter.org.uk/media/press_release/half_of_teachers_in_england_work_with_homeless_children.
24. Nicole Westmarland, Marianne Hester & Pam Reid, "Routine enquiry about domestic violence in general practices: a pilot project", School of Policy Studies, University of Bristol,2004. https://www.bristol.ac.uk/media-library/sites/sps/migrated/documents/rk6280finalreport.pdf.
25. Eight London boroughs, for example, run the IRIS (Identification and Referral to Improve Safety) programme of GP training for victim support and referrals in cases of domestic abuse.
26. Ruth Aitken & Vanessa Munro, *Domestic Abuse and Suicide: Exploring the Links with Refuge's Client Base and Work Force* (London: Refuge, 2018). https://wrap.warwick.ac.uk/103609/1/WRAP-Domestic-abuse-and-suicide-Munro-2018.pdf.
27. Mollie Malone, "'Staggering' number of domestic abuse victims taking own lives", Sky News, 25 March 2025. https://news.sky.com/story/staggering-number-of-domestic-abuse-victims-taking-own-lives-13335115.
28. Katherine Brickell, *Home SOS: Gender, Violence, and Survival in Crisis Ordinary Cambodia* (Chichester: John Wiley, 2020).
29. "Greater Manchester Police: an inspection of the service provided to victims of crime by Greater Manchester Police", His Majesty's Inspectorate of Constabulary and Fire and Rescue Services, December 2020. https://assets-hmicfrs.justiceinspectorates.gov.uk/uploads/an-inspection-of-the-service-provided-to-victims-of-crime-by-greater-manchester-police.pdf.
30. "New research shows police failing to act on domestic abuse reports: ethnic minority victims worst affected", Victim Support, 2022. https://www.victimsupport.org.uk/new-research-shows-police-failing-to-act-on-domestic-abuse-reports-ethnic-minority-victims-worst-affected/.
31. "Met Police: misogyny, racism, bullying, sex harassment discovered", BBC News, 1 February 2022. https://www.bbc.co.uk/news/uk-england-london-60215575; "Police are recruiting criminals and sexual predators, HMIC report finds", *The Times*, 2 November 2022. https://www.thetimes.com/uk/crime/article/police-organised-crime-vetting-officers-met-report-hmic-ks57flj96.
32. Dawsey-Hewitt *et al.*, "Shadow pandemic", 54.

33. Janet Bowstead, "Forced migration in the United Kingdom: women's journeys to escape domestic violence", *Transactions of the Institute of British Geographers* 40 (2015), 307–20.
34. Alston, "Press conference of the UN special rapporteur", 5.
35. Dana Cuomo & Natalie Dolci, "New tools, old abuse: technology-enabled coercive control (TECC)", *Geoforum* 126 (2021), 224, emphasis added.
36. Leonie Tanczer, Isabel Lopez-Neira, Simon Parkin, Trupti Patel & George Danezis, "Tech Abuse: Gender and IoT research report – the rise of the internet of things and implications for technology-facilitated abuse", University College London, November 2018. https://www.ucl.ac.uk/steapp/sites/steapp/files/giot-report.pdf.
37. Felicity Evans, "Domestic abuse survivor left with £10,000 debt after escaping", BBC News, 14 December 2023. https://www.bbc.co.uk/news/uk-wales-67705348.
38. Katherine Brickell & Mel Nowicki, "The debt trap: women's stories of navigating family homelessness and temporary accommodation in Greater Manchester", King's College London, 2023.
39. Dawsey-Hewitt *et al.*, "Shadow pandemic", 40.
40. Furnishing Futures Instagram post, 1 September 2024.
41. "Who is missing in the data? What the available data on domestic abuse does and doesn't tell us about women's experiences", Women's Aid, 8 March 2024. https://www.womensaid.org.uk/who-is-missing-in-the-data-what-the-available-data-on-domestic-abuse-does-and-doesnt-tell-us-about-womens-experiences/.
42. Naomi Graham & Katherine Brickell, "Sheltering from domestic violence: women's experiences of punitive safety and unfreedom in Cambodian safe shelters", *Gender, Place and Culture* 26:1 (2019), 112, emphasis in original.
43. Rhiannon James, "Domestic abuse is 'Cinderella' of crimes, safeguarding minister says", *The Independent*, 20 September 2024. https://www.independent.co.uk/news/uk/jess-phillips-yvette-cooper-cinderella-government-law-b2616153.html.
44. "Refuge responds to Autumn Budget announcement", Refuge, 31 October 2024. https://refuge.org.uk/news/refuge-responds-to-autumn-budget-announcement/.
45. A video of the session can be accessed via https://www.youtube.com/watch?v=Q9ggKkjZowQ.

4 IMPRISONED BY DEBT IN TEMPORARY ACCOMMODATION

1. "Statutory homelessness in England: July to September 2024", Ministry of Housing, Communities and Local Government. https://www.gov.uk/government/statistics/statutory-homelessness-in-england-july-to-september-2024/statutory-homelessness-in-england-july-to-september-2024.

2. Mel Nowicki, Katherine Brickell & Ella Harris, "The hotelisation of the housing crisis: experiences of family homelessness in Dublin hotels", *The Geographical Journal* 183:3 (2019), 313–24.
3. Ananya Roy, Gary Blasi, Johnny Coleman & Elana Eden, *Hotel California: Housing the Crisis* (Los Angeles: Institute on Inequality and Democracy, UCLA, 2020), 5.
4. This refers to a legal duty by a local authority to assess a person's housing needs and draw up a personalized housing plan if they are satisfied that the person is eligible for assistance and homeless or threatened with homelessness within 56 days.
5. "Statutory homelessness in England: July to September 2024", Ministry of Housing, Communities and Local Government.
6. "The Rightmove Rental Trends Tracker", Q3 2024 Report, Rightmove. https://www.rightmove.co.uk/news/content/uploads/2024/10/Rental-Trends-Tracker-Q3-2024-FINAL-1.pdf.
7. "People on Universal Credit could be as much as £670 worse off in April 2024 even if rates are increased in line with inflation", New Economics Foundation, press release, 18 October 2023. https://neweconomics.org/2023/10/people-on-universal-credit-could-be-as-much-as-670-worse-off-in-april-2024-even-if-rates-are-increased-in-line-with-inflation.
8. "Revealed: almost one million children in private housing face rent shortfall by 2026", Institute for Public Policy Research, 3 February 2025. https://www.ippr.org/media-office/revealed-almost-one-million-children-in-private-housing-face-rent-shortfall-by-2026.
9. "Only 5% of London private rentals affordable to low-income households, research finds", London Councils, 17 October 2024. https://www.londoncouncils.gov.uk/node/10947.
10. Donna Ferguson, "Nearly 1m children in UK at risk of poverty due to housing costs: report", *The Guardian*, 3 February 2025. https://www.theguardian.com/society/2025/feb/03/children-poverty-housing-costs-report-lha.
11. Tom Clark, "Sticking plaster politics and the sticky realities of the housing crisis", *Prospect*, 17 March 2025. https://www.prospectmagazine.co.uk/politics/labour-party/69536/sticking-plaster-politics-realities-of-housing-crisis-homelessness.
12. Bano, *Against Landlords*, 32.
13. "Young adult care leavers face 'appalling' higher risk of being homeless, charity says", Sky News, 29 October 2024. https://news.sky.com/story/young-adult-care-leavers-face-appalling-higher-risk-of-being-homeless-charity-says-13243629.
14. Amanda Sacker, Emily T. Murray, Barbara Maughan & Rebecca E. Lacey, "Social care in childhood and adult outcomes: double whammy for minority children?", *Longitudinal and Life Course Studies* 15:2 (2024), 139–62.
15. Department of Levelling Up, Housing and Communities, English Housing Survey 2021–2022. 13 July 2023: https://www.gov.uk/government/

statistics/english-housing-survey-2021-to-2022-private-rented-sector/english-housing-survey-2021-to-2022-private-rented-sector.

16. "English Housing Survey 2021–2022", Department for Levelling Up, Housing and Communities, 13 July 2023. https://www.gov.uk/government/statistics/english-housing-survey-2021-to-2022-private-rented-sector/english-housing-survey-2021-to-2022-private-rented-sector.
17. "Complain and you're out: research confirms link between tenant complaints and revenge eviction", Citizens Advice, 24 August 2018. https://www.citizensadvice.org.uk.cach3.com/wales/about-us/about-us1/media/press-releases/complain-and-youre-out-research-confirms-link-between-tenant-complaints-and-revenge-eviction/index.html%3Flang=cy.html.
18. Brickell, *Home SOS*.
19. Silvia Federici, "Women, money and debt: notes for a feminist reappropriation movement", *Australian Feminist Studies* 33:96 (2018), 181.
20. David Zucchino, *Myth of the Welfare Queen* (New York: Scriber, 1997).
21. Mel Nowicki, Katherine Brickell & Ella Harris, "Home at last? Everyday life in Dublin's rapid build housing", Dublin Housing Observatory, 2018. https://www.housingmodeldublin.ie/wp-content/uploads/Home_at_Last_report.pdf.
22. Here Taniyah is referring to the changing colour of the British passport. She has a burgundy passport that was issued from 1988 until the UK left the European Union in 2020. Since 2020 new passports are issued in blue. When she renews her passport, she will swap to a blue-coloured passport.
23. A "cracker" is a slave owner who "cracks the whip" to drive and punish slaves.
24. Briana Brownlow, "How racism 'gets under the skin': an examination of the physical- and mental-health costs of culturally compelled coping", *Perspectives on Psychological Science* 18:3 (2023), 576.
25. Spratt, "4,000 homeless families barred from social housing ... because they're in debt", *i Paper*, 24 October 2024. https://inews.co.uk/news/housing/homeless-families-barred-social-housing-debt-3339582.
26. Sheila Jasanoff, "Virtual, visible, and actionable: data assemblages and the sightlines of justice", *Big Data and Society* 4:2 (2017), emphasis in original. https://doi.org/10.1177/2053951717724477.
27. Leila Dawney, Samuel Kirwan & Rosie Walker, "The intimate spaces of debt: love, freedom and entanglement in indebted lives", *Geoforum* 110 (2020), 191–9.
28. *Rethinking Allocations*, Chartered Institute of Housing, 2019, 4. https://www.cih.org/media/ezugl10q/rethinking-allocations.pdf.
29. "Real life roomsets, Sam's story", IKEA. https://www.ikea.com/gb/en/this-is-ikea/community-engagement/real-life-roomsets-ikea-hammersmith-pub08924350.

5 FAMILY LIVES CAUGHT IN COSTLY LIMBO

1. London Councils, *London's Homelessness Emergency* (2024), 3. https://www.londoncouncils.gov.uk/sites/default/files/2024-10/londons_homelessness_emergency_october_2024.pdf.
2. The interview took place in November 2024 online. The IKEA–Shelter partnership runs until 2030 and includes corporate funding to Shelter's frontline services.
3. In each store one real person's story was the centrepiece of the roomset. In the London store, this was Sam's. She visited it with her children and met the IKEA team behind the roomset.
4. Diana Margot Rosenthal, Antoinette Schoenthaler, Michelle Heys, Marcella Ucci, Andrew Hayward, Ashlee Teakle, Monica Lakhanpaul & Celine Lewis, "How does living in temporary accommodation and the COVID-19 pandemic impact under 5s' healthcare access and health outcomes? A qualitative study of key professionals in a socially and ethnically diverse and deprived area of London", *International Journal of Environmental Research and Public Health* 20:2 (2023), 1300.
5. Nowicki, Brickell & Harris, "The hotelisation of the housing crisis", 319.
6. "Homes with kitchens for all our children", The Magpie Project. https://themagpieproject.org/hope-for-a-home-with-a-kitchen/.
7. *Ibid.*
8. "Temporary Accommodation Conference 2023", Justlife, 25 October 2023. https://www.justlife.org.uk/news/2023/temporary-accommodation-conference-2023.
9. Scott Corfe, "What are the barriers to eating healthy in the UK?" The Social Market Foundation, 2018. https://www.smf.co.uk/wp-content/uploads/2018/10/What-are-the-barriers-to-eating-healthy-in-the-UK.pdf.
10. Sally Lockwood, "1.2 million people too far from supermarkets to get cheap fresh food", Sky News, 12 October 2018. https://news.sky.com/story/uk-food-deserts-1-2-million-people-too-far-from-supermarkets-to-get-cheap-fresh-food-11523391.
11. Other women also spoke highly of "The Bread and Butter Thing", which offers £35 worth of shopping for £8.50 per week. https://www.breadandbutterthing.org.
12. Jack Fifield, "Appeal for donations as Oldham food bank struggles", *Oldham Times*, 4 August 2023. https://www.theoldhamtimes.co.uk/news/23699725.appeal-donations-oldham-food-bank-struggles/.
13. Richardson & Butler, *The Single Parent Debt Trap*.
14. "Exclusive: 55 homeless children have died in temporary accommodation since 2019", Shared Health Foundation, 5 March 2024. https://sharedhealthfoundation.org.uk/news/exclusive-55-homeless-children-have-died-in-temporary-accommodation-since-2019/.
15. "Child mortality in temporary accommodation 2025", All-Party

Parliamentary Group for Households in Temporary Accommodation, 28 January 2025. https://householdsintemporaryaccommodation.co.uk/reports/child-mortality-in-temporary-accommodation-2025/.

16. SIDS – sometimes known as "cot death" – is the sudden, unexpected and unexplained death of an apparently healthy baby. Most deaths occur in children under six months. Risk of SIDS is vastly reduced if babies have access to a safe sleep environment: on their back, in a clear cot.
17. Wendy Wilson, "Constituency casework: does the law set a minimum bedroom size in England?", House of Commons Library, 2 May 2023. https://commonslibrary.parliament.uk/does-the-law-set-a-minimum-bedroom-size-in-england/.
18. "Safer sleep advice for babies", Lullaby Trust. https://www.lullabytrust.org.uk/baby-safety/safer-sleep-information/safer-sleep-overview/.
19. Geraghty, "Council spending on homelessness triples in eight years".
20. "Before Our Eyes", Amnesty International. https://www.amnesty.org.uk/before-our-eyes.
21. Judith Butler, *Frames of War: When Is Life Grievable?* (London: Verso, 2009).
22. "Before Our Eyes", Amnesty International.
23. Grainne Cuffe, "Awaab's Law will extend to temporary accommodation, minister announces", *Inside Housing*, 25 February 2025. https://www.insidehousing.co.uk/news/awaabs-law-will-extend-to-temporary-accommodation-minister-announces-90709.
24. Cathrine Brun & Anita Fábos, "Making homes in limbo? A conceptual framework", *Refuge* 31:5 (2015), 9.
25. "Homelessness Code of Guidance for Local Authorities", Ministry of Housing, Communities and Local Government. https://www.gov.uk/guidance/homelessness-code-of-guidance-for-local-authorities/chapter-9-intentional-homelessness.
26. Kate Belgrave, "Intentionally homeless with kids? Council will house the kids but not you – ie, you'll be separated from them. The hell with this". 4 February 2018. https://www.katebelgrave.com/2018/02/intentionally-homeless-with-kids-council-will-house-the-kids-but-not-you-ie-youll-be-separated-from-them-the-hell-with-this/.
27. Mary Douglas, *Purity and Danger* (London: Routledge, 2002 [1966]), 44.
28. Ben Campkin & Rosie Cox (eds), *Dirt: New Geographies of Cleanliness and Contamination* (London: Bloomsbury, 2012).
29. Michael Marmot, Jessica Allen, Peter Goldblatt, Tammy Boyce, Di McNeish, Mike Grady & Ilaria Geddes, *Fair Society, Healthy Lives* (The Marmot Review), Institute of Health Equity, February 2010. https://www.instituteofhealthequity.org/resources-reports/fair-society-healthy-lives-the-marmot-review.
30. Awaab Ishak, "Guidance on mould to be reviewed after toddler's death", BBC News, 14 January 2023. https://www.bbc.co.uk/news/uk-64273057#.

31. Edward Kirton-Darling, "Death, social reform and the scrutiny of social welfare provision: the role of the contemporary inquest", *Journal of Social Welfare and Family Law* 45:4 (2023), 363–86.
32. Peter Apps, "The office-to-residential conversions which have become slum housing", *Inside Housing*, 2 January 2024. https://www.insidehousing.co.uk/insight/the-office-to-residential-conversions-which-have-become-slum-housing-84138.
33. "Still living in limbo: why the use of temporary accommodation must end", Shelter (2023). https://tfl.ams3.cdn.digitaloceanspaces.com/media/documents/Still_Living_in_Limbo.pdf.
34. Vicky Spratt, "Conditions for homeless families living in office blocks 'deeply concerning', says Michael Gove", *i News*, 21 February 2023. https://inews.co.uk/news/conditions-homeless-families-living-office-blocks-michael-gove-2150689.
35. Apps, "The office-to-residential conversions which have become slum housing".
36. Jon Ungoed-Thomas, "Labour condemned for allowing 'new generation of slum homes' in England", *The Guardian*, 14 December 2024. https://www.theguardian.com/society/2024/dec/14/labour-condemned-for-allowing-new-generation-of-slum-homes-in-england.
37. "Change it! 'It's like being in prison': children speak out on homelessness", Children's Rights Alliance, 2018. https://crae.org.uk/sites/default/files/uploads/462614-CRAE_CHANGE-IT-REPORT-Digital-final.pdf.
38. Georgia Poncia and Lauren Woodhead, "'Don't just throw us on the streets after prison'", BBC News, 9 September 2024. https://www.bbc.co.uk/news/articles/cj08g87r8j4o.
39. In this respect, Stephanie was relatively "lucky", as not all local authorities have warehouses.
40. Street Storage. https://www.streetstorage.org/.
41. We met Elizabeth together in October 2016 before she had moved to PLACE/Ladywell. We then met her in the PLACE/Ladywell temporary accommodation in March 2017. Several years later, during the Covid-19 pandemic in May 2020, we interviewed her for a third time via phone.
42. PLACE/Ladywell is pioneering temporary accommodation developed by Lewisham Council, London, in partnership with the architecture company Roger Stirk Harbour + Partners. It uses off-site manufacturing processes to provide modular, mobile housing units, in use as temporary accommodation for 24 homeless families. For more information of our work with its residents, see Ella Harris, Katherine Brickell & Mel Nowicki, *Temporary Homes, Permanent Progress?* Resident Experiences of PLACE/Ladywell, 2019. https://pure.royalholloway.ac.uk/ws/portalfiles/portal/34520821/LewishamReport_FINAL_Sep_2019.pdf.
43. "How much are self storage prices in 2024?", Comparemymove. https://www.comparemymove.com/advice/storage/self-storage-unit-costs.

44. Howard Jacob Karger, "The 'Poverty Tax' and America's low-income households", *Families in Society* 88:3 (2007), 413–17.
45. "Mainstream home to school transport and college transport policy", Oldham Council, February 2022. https://www.oldham.gov.uk/homepage/1407/mainstream_home_to_school_transport_and_college_transport_policy.html.
46. Shelter, "Still living in limbo".
47. "Apply for a secondary school travel pass", Manchester City Council. https://www.manchester.gov.uk/info/100005/schools_education_and_childcare/7051/apply_for_a_secondary_school_travel_pass.
48. "Travel to school for children of compulsory school age: statutory guidance for local authorities", Department for Education. https://www.gov.uk/government/publications/home-to-school-travel-and-transport-guidance.

6 SHIT HOUSING: DEBT BEYOND HOMELESSNESS IN A FAILING STATE

1. "Refusing an offer of an unsuitable council home", Citizens Advice. https://www.citizensadvice.org.uk/wales/housing/applying-for-council-housing-or-a-housing-association-home/refusing-an-offer-of-an-unsuitable-council-home-w/.
2. In December 2024, we were invited to a university in Frankfurt, Germany to present our research. In the Q&A session, a student remarked that Britain had a reputation for what she described as "shit housing", especially in the rental sector. The word "shit" is commonplace in the interview transcripts from the project, and it was telling that although we didn't use this word in our presentation, the swear word was used in response to it.
3. Will Hutton, "The bad news is we're dying early in Britain – and it's all down to 'shit-life syndrome'", *The Guardian*, 19 August 2018. https://www.theguardian.com/commentisfree/2018/aug/19/bad-news-is-were-dying-earlier-in-britain-down-to-shit-life-syndrome.
4. Maurizio Lazzarato, *The Making of the Indebted Man: An Essay on the Neoliberal Condition* (Cambridge, MA: MIT Press, 2012).
5. Helen Garrett, Susie Margoles, Molly Mackay & Simon Nicol, "The cost of poor housing tenure in England: 2023 briefing paper – tenure based analysis", Building Research Establishment (2023). https://files.bregroup.com/corporate/BRE_cost%20of%20poor%20housing%20tenure%20analysis%202023.pdf.
6. "115,000 of London's social homes fail to meet decent standards", Mayor of London, 17 February 2022. https://www.london.gov.uk/press-releases/mayoral/mayor-demands-social-housing-step change.
7. "Housing Ombudsman's Annual Complaints Review reveals 22,000 interventions made to put things right for residents", Housing Ombudsman

Service press release, 5 November 2024. https://www.housing-ombudsman.org.uk/2024/11/05/annual-complaints-review/.

8. Fiona Trott & Ruth Green, "Complaints about rats in social housing rise", BBC News, 20 December 2023. https://www.bbc.co.uk/news/uk-67727079.
9. Anne-Marie Bancroft, Bekah Ryder, Mihir Shah, Will Morley & Rebecca How, "The provision of floor coverings in social housing", Longleigh Foundation, May 2024. https://longleigh.org/wp-content/uploads/2024/05/Final-Report-Longleigh-Flooring-v2.pdf.
10. "Floored: provision of appropriate flooring in social housing", Tenant Participation Advisory Service Cymru & Tai Pawb, 22 October 2020. https://www.tpas.cymru/ckfinder/userfiles/files/FLOORED%20-%20FULL%20final%20report(1).pdf.
11. "The Welsh Housing Quality Standard 2023: maintaining and improving social housing in Wales", Gov.Wales, April 2023. https://www.gov.wales/sites/default/files/publications/2024-06/welsh-housing-quality-standard-2023.pdf.
12. "Single families impact report", One Parent Families Scotland. https://opfs.org.uk/wp-content/uploads/2023/04/OPFS-Impact-Report_Pre-paid_meters_and_self_disconnection.pdf.
13. Richardson & Butler, *The Single Parent Debt Trap*, 6.
14. Citizens Advice, "Debt time bomb".
15. *Autumn Budget 2024*, Gov.UK, 30 October 2024. https://www.gov.uk/government/publications/autumn-budget-2024/autumn-budget-2024-html.
16. "Universal Credit rent deductions scheme declared unlawful by High Court", Garden Court Chambers, 17 January 2025. https://gcnchambers.co.uk/universal-credit-rent-deductions-scheme-declared-unlawful-by-high-court/.
17. Joseph Spooner, "Levelling up or knocking down? How the crisis of council tax debt is experienced across English local authorities", LSE blog, 8 February 2023. https://eprints.lse.ac.uk/122312/.
18. Citizens Advice, "Debt time bomb".
19. Murray & Smith, "In the public interest?".
20. Indirect taxes refer to those levied on services and goods rather than incomes and profits.
21. "Effects of taxes and benefits on UK household income: financial year ending 2022", Office for National Statistics. https://www.ons.gov.uk/peoplepopulationandcommunity/personalandhouseholdfinances/incomeandwealth/bulletins/theeffectsoftaxesandbenefitsonhouseholdincome/financialyearending2022.
22. Ellie Simmonds, "Inflation on budget groceries outstrips other food and drink", Which?, 19 November 2023. https://www.which.co.uk/news/article/inflation-on-budget-groceries-outstrips-other-food-and-drink-awFOS1I07xXX.
23. Alston, "I proved that austerity destroys lives".

7 EPILOGUE: DISMANTLING THE DEBT TRAP

1. Furnishing Futures, a London-based charity, harnesses trauma-informed design in their work to furnish the social housing of women domestic violence victims. We interviewed its founder in September 2024.
2. Ruth Patrick, "Social security is not a burden: it's a force for good", *Prospect*, 12 March 2025. https://www.prospectmagazine.co.uk/society/poverty/69511/social-security-is-not-a-burden-disability-benefits-cuts-starmer.
3. Imogen Tyler & Sarah Campbell, "Poverty stigma: a glue that holds poverty in place", Joseph Rowntree Foundation, 8 May 2024. https://www.jrf.org.uk/sites/default/files/pdfs/poverty-stigma-a-glue-that-holds-poverty-in-place-bbc1fd2874559e6d2b9a1dccff6ddb7b.pdf.
4. StepChange and The Children's Society, *The Debt Trap*, 2.

A NOTE ON RESEARCH METHODS

1. See Rooftop Illustrations. https://www.rooftopillustrations.net.
2. Brickell & Nowicki, *The Debt Trap*.
3. See Anthony Luvera. https://www.luvera.com.

Index

Note: Page numbers in *italics* indicate figures.